The
BREATH
of Life

A WORKBOOK

The
BREATH
of Life

A Simple Way to Pray

A WORKBOOK

Ron DelBene
with Mary & Herb Montgomery

UPPER
ROOM BOOKS
Nashville

Unless otherwise indicated scripture quotations are from The New Revised Standard Version of the Bible, copyright © 1989 by the Division of Christian Education of the National Council of the Churches of Christ in the United States of America. Used by permission.

Scripture quotations identified as JB are from *The Jerusalem Bible,* copyright © 1966, 1967, and 1968 by Darton, Longman & Todd Ltd. and Doubleday & Co. Inc., and used by permission of the publishers.

The publisher gratefully acknowledges permission to reprint the following copyrighted material:

Excerpts from *The Art of Prayer,* compiled by Igumen Chariton of Valmo, translated by E. Kadloubovsky and E. M. Palmer. Copyright © 1966 by Elizabeth M. Palmer. Used by permission of Faber & Faber, Ltd.

Excerpts from *Meditations with Julian of Norwich,* by Brendan Doyle, copyright © 1983, Bear & Co., Sante Fe, NM. Used by permission of the publisher.

Excerpts from *Meditations with Mechtild of Magdeburg,* by Sue Woodruff, copyright © 1982, Bear & Co., Sante Fe, NM. Used by permission of the publisher.

Excerpts from *Psalms Anew: In Inclusive Language,* by Nancy Schreck and Maureen Leach. St. Mary's Press, Winona, MN, 1986. Used by permission of the publisher.

Excerpts from *Meditations with Teresa of Avila,* by Camille Campbell, copyright © 1985, Bear & Co., Sante Fe, NM. Used by permission of the publisher.

Excerpts from *Writing from the Philokalia on Prayer of the Heart,* translated by E. Kadloubovsky and G. E. H. Palmer, 1979, © 1951. Used by permission of Faber & Faber, Ltd.

Cover design by Gore Studio, Inc.
Cover photograph by Westlight © Chuck O'Rear
First Printing: March 1995 (7)
ISBN: 0-8358-0766-5
Printed in the United States of America

To all those
who have shared their lives
with me in prayer

ALSO BY THE AUTHORS

Christmas Remembered
From the Heart

Into the Light Collection
Into the Light
When I'm Alone
Near Life's End
A Time to Mourn (also on cassette)
Study Guide

Times of Change, Times of Challenge Series
When You Are Getting Married
When Your Child Is Baptized
When You Are Facing Surgery
When an Aging Loved One Needs Care
When You Have a Decision to Make
When You Are Living with an Illness That Is Not Your Own
When Your Son or Daughter Divorces
When You Want Your Wishes Known: Wills and
Other Final Arrangements

Breath of Life Series
The Breath of Life
The Breath of Life Workbook
The Hunger of the Heart
The Hunger of the Heart Workbook
Alone with God

Video Series by Ron DelBene
Praying in the Midst of Life
Our Questions about Prayer
Finding God
Knowing God's Will
Praying the Scripture
Learning the Breath Prayer
Retreating at Any Time

Contents

ABOUT THIS WORKBOOK

The Breath of Life: A Simple Way to Pray was first published in 1981. It initiated The Breath of Life Series, which also includes *The Hunger of the Heart: A Call to Spiritual Growth* and *Alone with God: A Guide for Personal Retreats*.

Over the years *The Breath of Life* has been popular in groups where people meet to pray together and share their spiritual journey. Many who used the book in this way expressed interest in a guide that would give more structure to their time together and include questions to help focus their discussions. Instead of a guide, my coauthors and I created this workbook. Along with the content of *The Breath of Life*, it includes daily reflections, exercises, and guidelines for group meetings.

The time to bring out the workbook had arrived after the release of my video series *Praying in the Midst of Life*. That series includes "Learning the Breath Prayer," which you will view at the first meeting of your study group. Through the medium of the video, I am able to be a part of your group just as so many spiritual seekers have been a part of my life through their friendship and the stories they have shared.

An important part of my ministry is spiritual direction. I encourage those who seek my guidance to keep a journal, which they in turn share with me. These deeply felt writings reveal what happens when we choose to let God enter more fully into our lives. *The Breath of Life* includes a number of journal entries, all of which are used with permission. The entries appear as written, but in the interest of privacy, we have changed names and some identifying details. The hope of those who agreed to let us use their entries is that others will benefit from their experiences.

Quotations about prayer and the spiritual life appear throughout *The Breath of Life* and in this workbook. For the most part they were written in times when the male pronoun referred to both male and female and was used exclusively in reference to God. We selected the quotations with the belief that what the writers have to say is of such value that readers will not let the noninclusive language get in the way of the message.

People seldom ask us "What is your deepest yearning?" This program both asks the question and helps you find the answer. Whether or not you have read *The Breath of Life*, the readings and exercises in this workbook will open you to discoveries about yourself and heighten your awareness of God's presence in your life. Through sharing with other companions on the way, you will gain ideas for growing in the Spirit and receive encouragement to continue the journey that takes you closer to God.

Ron DelBene

GROUP MEETING GUIDELINES

The Breath of Life Workbook has five weekly group sessions and individual daily exercises for twenty-four days. Group sessions are designed to last from forty-five minutes to an hour and a half. Those participating in the program are asked to commit themselves to praying daily, doing the readings and reflections, and attending the group sessions—understanding, of course, that circumstances sometimes make that impossible.

A group of eight to twelve members is a good size. If you are starting with a larger group than that, form smaller groups. When a group is too large, it is difficult for everyone to share and participate in the discussion. Because group members will explore and reflect on their faith journey in preparation for the weekly meetings, discussions are likely to be more personal and filled with more of their own stories than might be the case in other groups.

Establish when and where you will hold the meetings. If you use the program within a regular church curriculum, the meeting place will probably be predetermined. Otherwise groups typically meet in church classrooms or parlors or in private homes. When meetings are held in a home, make sure directions to the house are clear and that interruptions (children, pets, telephone) can be kept to a minimum.

There are, however, other possibilities for meeting places. Groups sometimes meet for lunch at a restaurant where they can use a private room for their meeting. Business people often get together for an early breakfast and sharing.

For the first meeting, it is necessary to have a VCR. If the site you have chosen does not have a VCR available, hold your first meeting where you have access to one. Thereafter you may meet elsewhere.

One person from the group can act as the leader for the entire program or a new leader can be assigned from week to week. Make this decision before or at the first meeting of the group.

If you choose to serve refreshments (food and/or beverages) at the beginning of your time together, do not let it delay starting the meeting. Serve refreshments at the end of the meeting only if you are certain that most of the people can stay most of the time. It does not enhance the group spirit if, on a regular basis, some people have to leave while others are free to stay and continue the discussion.

This program is not so much about prayer as it is about praying and becoming more aware of, and responsive to, God's presence in the midst of life. Throughout the week everyone in the group uses the same prayer, inserting the name of the week's prayer companion. (See Step 6 in First Group Meeting.) Members of the group also pray their breath prayer, then reflect on it as a means of developing their awareness of God's action in their lives. Prayer is a powerful means of uniting us. As we prayerfully enter into the sacred journey of others and share our own, we have the sense of being on holy ground.

GROUP LEADERS:

- Arrange the room ahead of time and have the necessary materials on hand. You may want to have a focus area: a Bible as a reminder that we live in the presence of God's word, a candle as a reminder that Jesus is the light of the world, flowers or a plant as a reminder that we are all part of a world that is growing and changing.

- Be warm and welcoming to everyone in the group. Name tags help people feel comfortable with one another. Even though people may be acquainted already, have name tags in the event someone brings a guest. Name tags encased in plastic and pinned on can be made at the first meeting and worn thereafter.

- Be willing to share your personal experiences. Sharing an experience of your own encourages others to do the same.

- Encourage everyone to participate. If one or two people tend to dominate the discussion, invite others to contribute.

- Center the discussion on personal experiences. Avoid controversial issues that have the potential for becoming only an intellectual debate.

- Use a watch or timer to time silent prayer and reflections.

- Keep to the time schedule. If the meeting is running late, get a consensus from the group before continuing beyond the designated time.

- Make these points at every meeting:

  (1) Each of us has a different view and is at a different place in our prayer life.

  (2) There is no one way that God calls a person and no single right way to respond in prayer.

FIRST GROUP MEETING

PURPOSE:

To get acquainted and to introduce *The Breath of Life* program.

MATERIALS NEEDED:

- The video *Learning the Breath Prayer,* TV, and VCR for showing it
- Name tags
- A workbook for each member of the group
- A 3 x 5 index card for each member of the group (See Step 6.)
- Watch or timer
- Bible, candle in a sturdy holder, plant or fresh flowers

PREPARATIONS:

- Have the video ready to show.
- Arrange the seating so people can see the video easily. (After the viewing you may want to rearrange the seating in a circle so people can see one another.)
- Create a focal point with the Bible, candle, and plant or flowers. Have the Bible open and the candle lit as people arrive.

PROCEDURE:

➤ 1. Begin with a get-acquainted exercise. Explain that the group will begin its time together with one minute of silence during which group members are to think about why they felt called to the *The Breath of Life* program. Ask this question:

- What drew you to these sessions?

(Use a watch or timer.) After the minute is up, introduce yourself and share your response to the question. What you say will set the tone for the others, so keep your sharing brief and focused. Turn to the person on your right (or left) and say, "Let's go around the group in this direction."

➤ 2. When everyone has shared, pray this prayer:

Thank you, God, for bringing us together
on this journey that takes
us deeper into a life of prayer.
Guide us to look within
that we might discover our deepest needs
and place them in your hands.
Grant us the grace to know
that you are with us always
and to feel your
loving presence in our lives.
Amen.

(This prayer is the same one you will pray together at the end of the meeting when group members have their workbooks.)

➤ 3. Show the video *Learning the Breath Prayer.* It introduces Ron DelBene, author of the book *The Breath of Life* and this workbook. (The video takes 21 minutes viewing time.)

➤ 4. Discussion questions to use after viewing the video:

- As you listened to the people in the video discuss their experience with prayer, with whom did you most identify? (Vince, Terrence, Pablo, Barbara, Janet)

- What do you think about praying in the way introduced in the video?

- When during the day could you remember to be aware of God's presence?

➤ 5. If group members do not already have their workbooks, hand them out now. Make these points:

- Before beginning Week 1, Day 1 in the workbook, read "When God's Time and Our Time Intersect." This reading welcomes members of the group on their journey into prayer.

- The workbook has four weeks of daily exercises. Each day begins with a prayer of thanksgiving for companions on the way. (See Step 6.)

Repetition of the breath prayer follows. Beginning the second week, there is also an invitation to reflect on and record insights that occur as we are attentive to prayer and God's presence.

- Each daily exercise has a reading from *The Breath of Life*. The reading is followed by an activity that takes twenty to thirty minutes.

➤ 6. Pass out index cards and ask each member of the group to write his or her name on one. Place the cards face down and mix them up. Each person then draws a card. Those who get their own name draw again. The name on the card is the person they will pray for specifically in the coming week. They are to write the name in the space provided in the prayer that begins each day. (Save the cards. Each week reshuffle them and draw new names.)

➤ 7. Invite members of the group to bring a symbol that has relevance to their prayer life and put it on the focus table. In the discussion part of the meeting they will have an opportunity to share the meaning the symbol has for them. Respect the fact that for some people bringing the symbol is all the sharing they care to do.

➤ 8. Close with prayer. Use the prayer that opened the meeting. By revisiting the prayer after sharing has occurred, the group is likely to find new meaning in it. Ask everyone to turn to this page and together pray:

Thank you, God, for bringing us together
on this journey that takes
us deeper into a life of prayer.
Guide us to look within
that we might discover our deepest needs
and place them in your hands.
Grant us the grace to know
that you are with us always
and to feel your
loving presence in our lives.
Amen.

NOTES

INTRODUCTION

When God's Time and Our Time Intersect

The following reading welcomes you on your journey into prayer. Read it after the first group meeting and before starting the reading for Week 1, Day 1.

Often things happen to us that have a meaning we do not understand at the time. Yet we know that something of unusual importance has occurred. We may be sitting with a friend or reading or listening to music or walking alone in nature when something alerts us. Like Moses at the burning bush, we proceed carefully, aware that we are on holy ground. God's time and our time intersect, and we have the gift to know it.

These experiences are not as rare as some would have us think. Based on my own life and what others have shared with me, I have come to believe that an awareness of God's time and our time intersecting is not only a possibility—it is something we are called to be aware of. My own life has included a number of such experiences. As I share a few of them, you may feel that some or all of them are quite ordinary. Indeed, they may be, but while each occurred I was aware of myself and my God in a mysterious and beautiful way.

I was an adult before I could share how, as a young boy, I knelt in a candle-lit mission church in a small Ohio city and knew that I had seen into heaven, but I dared not say so to anyone. God's time and my time had intersected, and as a child, I had the gift to know it.

Another incident occurred one Sunday evening in October 1963. The weekend retreat I had attended was over, and those of us who participated were visiting in the church basement. It had been a powerful weekend, and I sensed that all of us were feeling especially close to God. I happened to be standing next to a scruffy elderly man who had been brought to the retreat by the retreat leader. The leader's ministry included working with inmates at the county jail. When he was giving a retreat, he would request that certain regulars at the jail be released to his custody. I began talking with the gentleman from the jail, and at one point tears filmed his eyes. With great emotion in his voice, he said, "Why, *oh why*, did it take so long for me to have this experience with God?"

From the core of my being and matching his intensity of emotion, I said, "And why has it happened to me so *early*? When I am so *young*?" In that moment I had a flash of awareness that my journey was lifelong and that I had been called to be attentive for all my days. God's time and my time had again intersected.

Yet another incident occurred when I was a graduate student studying theology and having a difficult time reconciling my textbook studies with the social justice activity of the mid-sixties. In trying to decide whether to cut back on my classes and become more involved in social justice ministry, I went to talk to one of my professors. He was someone in whom I had great confidence and with whom I had previously shared what was happening in my life. At one point in our conversation there was a silence, and he said, "Let's pray the Lord's Prayer together." As I said the words *Our Father* I began to weep, and the pieces of all the issues I had been dealing with began to come together. God's power was present. *And I knew it.*

Again, on my wedding day, I felt God's presence in a special way. As I waited to go down the aisle, I glanced off to the right. There was Eleanor coming through an archway, the whole of which shone with light. The overwhelming presence of beauty that I sensed at that moment has remained throughout the many years of our marriage.

A common thread runs through these experiences. In each of them my heart was touched, opened, and examined. At those times I *knew* what the psalmist meant by "Yahweh, you examine me and know me" (Psalm 139:1, JB).

As I have traveled my own journey of the Spirit and as others have shared their journeys with me, I have come to believe that *we all have the gift of knowing when God's time and our time intersect.* After I had made this point at a conference, a young man came up afterward and said, "I want to know more about this gift of knowing. What do you base it on? Is there some foundation?"

"What I believe," I told him, "is that God is present to us, and we are in God's presence in every action of our lives. Becoming aware of this is spiritual growth, and living as attentively as possible in that reality is what life is all about."

There are many approaches to living in God's presence, and in the readings in *The Breath of Life Workbook* I share mine. To begin, I ask that you look at your own life.

- When have you had an experience that awakened your inner spirit?

- Did you feel that you were in some way on holy ground?

- Were you so touched by the experience that you tucked it away in your heart, not sharing it with anyone?

If the life of the Spirit is new to you, or if prayer is new to you, or if for any other reason you feel that your time and God's time have not intersected, be patient. In *The Breath of Life* program, we are companions on the way—companions on a journey that takes us deeper into the life of the Spirit. On this journey the breath prayer will help you feel God's presence not just in extraordinary occurrences but in the ordinariness of everyday life.

NOTES

Week One, Day One

PRAYER:

> God of all creation, I give thanks that I am united in your breath
> with _____ and all those joined in this journey
> into prayer. May each of us become more aware of your loving
> presence in our lives.   Amen.

> Center yourself by praying your breath prayer five times.
>
> If you do not yet have a breath prayer, use
>
> "O God, let me feel your presence."

- After your prayer, be aware of your body. If you are tense, take several deep breaths to relax.

- Be aware of God's presence.

- Recall the reason you gave at the group meeting for taking part in this program. Were there reasons you did not share? Write your reason(s) for taking part in the program here: _____

_____

_____

READING FOR TODAY:

Today's reading reviews the video from the first group meeting. If you have not yet discovered your breath prayer, you have an opportunity to do it now. If you have your prayer, you may want to "touch it up" until you are satisfied that it express- es your deepest yearning and flows easily when spoken aloud or is expressed as a heart thought.

DISCOVERING YOUR BREATH PRAYER

The breath prayer lies within us like a tiny seed that, when nurtured, flowers into a new and deeper awareness of God's presence. To discover your breath prayer, follow these five easy steps:

STEP ONE

Sit in a comfortable position. Close your eyes, and remind yourself that God loves you and that you are in God's loving presence. Recall a passage from scripture that puts you in a prayerful frame of mind. Consider "The Lord is my shepherd" (Psalm 23:1) or "Be still, and know that I am God!" (Psalm 46:10).

STEP TWO

With your eyes closed, imagine that God is calling you by name. Hear God ask- ing, "*(Your name)*, what do you want?"

STEP THREE

Answer God with whatever comes directly from your heart. Your answer might be a single word, such as *peace* or *love* or *forgiveness.* Your answer could instead be a phrase or brief sentence, such as "I want to feel your forgiveness" or "I want to know your love."

Because the prayer is personal, it naturally rises out of our present con- cerns. One person may focus on physical health, another on becoming peace- ful within, still another on learning to hear God's voice more clearly or being released from guilt. Your response to God's question "What do you want?" becomes the heart of your prayer.

STEP FOUR

Choose your favorite name or image for God. Choices commonly made include God, Jesus, Creator, Teacher, Light, Lord, Spirit, Shepherd.

STEP FIVE

Combine your name for God with your answer to God's question "What do you want?" You then have your prayer. For example:

What I Want	Name I Call God	Possible Prayer
peace	God	Let me know your peace, O God.
love	Jesus	Jesus, let me feel your love.
rest	Shepherd	My Shepherd, let me rest in thee.
guidance	Eternal Light	Eternal Light, guide me in your way.

What do you do if several ideas occur? Write down the various possibilities and then eliminate and/or combine ideas until you have focused your prayer. You may want many things, but it is possible to narrow wants to those most basic to your well-being. Thus, the question to ask yourself is *What do I want that will make me feel most whole?* As you achieve a greater feeling of wholeness, serenity will flow into the many areas of your life.

When you have gotten to the heart of your deep yearning, search for words that give it expression. Then work with the words until you have a prayer of six to eight syllables that flows smoothly when spoken aloud or expressed as a heart thought. A prayer of six to eight syllables has a natural rhythm. Anything longer or shorter usually does not flow easily when said repeatedly.

Some prayers are more rhythmic when you place God's name at the beginning; other prayers flow better with it at the end. Sometimes rearranging the words gives the prayer rhythm. For instance, "God, let me know your peace" may be more rhythmic for you by changing it to "Let me know your peace, O God." When your prayer seems right for you, use it again and again throughout the day.

Whatever your prayer, it needs to be *your own*. Several years ago at a conference some of the people chose to share their breath prayers with one another. I heard such prayers as "Jesus, lead my son to you" and "Bless my family, Lord." While these prayers are fine, they are not what the breath prayer is about. When Jesus said to the blind man, "What do you want?" the man did not say, "Lord, that I may see so that I can make a living and support others." No, the question drew from the blind man his deepest yearning—the yearning that would make him feel most whole—and he said, "Lord, that I may see." Likewise, when you hear Jesus ask, "What do you want?" respond with whatever expresses *your* deepest yearning. Although you may feel you are being selfish, speak the true desire of your heart. That, then, becomes your breath prayer—a prayer that is your first step toward praying unceasingly and feeling the nearness of God.

REFLECTING AND RESPONDING

Write your breath prayer here:

_____

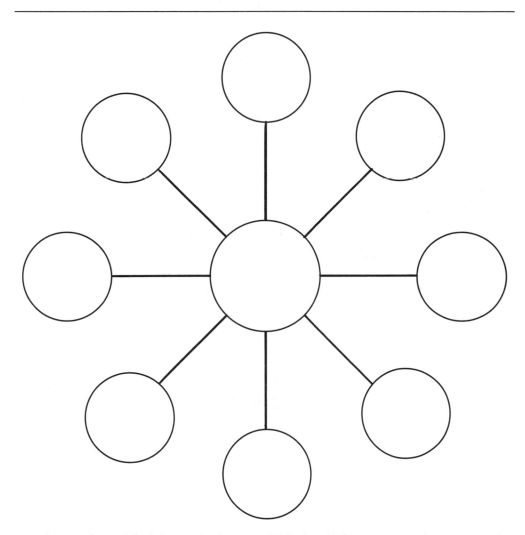

Write your deepest yearning in the center circle. In the outer circles, write other desires you have at this point in your life. Do they relate to one another? Do you see a pattern evolving? What does a pattern or lack of pattern tell you about your life?

Week One, Day Two

❦

PRAYER:

> God of all creation, I give thanks that I am united in your breath with _____ and all those joined in this journey into prayer. May each of us become more aware of your loving presence in our lives. Amen.

⤳ Center yourself by praying your breath prayer five times. ⤳

- After your prayer, be aware of your body. If you are tense, take several deep breaths to relax.
- Be aware of God's presence as you journey deeper into a life of prayer.

Reading for today:

Questions about the Breath Prayer

When I introduce the breath prayer at a conference or seminar on spiritual growth, questions usually follow. I always feel gratified by this because it lets me know that the people in the audience are serious and discerning—unwilling to take up a spiritual discipline unless they feel it has merit and is right for them. Following are some typically asked questions and my responses to them.

Is it possible that I am already using a breath prayer?

After I have taught the breath prayer, people frequently tell me that they have used such a prayer without calling it that. What I usually discover, however, is that these people do not stay with a specific prayer very long. Instead they tend to alternate their prayers or use crisis prayers whenever a serious problem arises. I encourage those who have used a number of such prayers to go back through the process and discover their most basic response to God's question: "(*Your name*), what do you want?" Then I urge them to stay with that prayer. Staying with a single prayer that expresses our deepest need is a helpful way to focus on God's power and love.

Once I begin using the breath prayer, what happens to my other prayers?

The breath prayer is not intended to replace your other prayers or your ways of expressing them. I liken prayer life to a house that includes many parts, all of which require a foundation. Think of the place where you live. Each room serves a purpose. While cooking in the kitchen, sleeping in the bedroom, or gathering with friends in the living area, you give little thought to the supporting foundation—unless, of course, it is faulty! Normally we assume the foundation is solid, doing what it is intended to do. The breath prayer can serve as the foundation upon which you build your life of prayer.

Immediately after discovering your breath prayer, you might find it so new and exciting that it is more like an addition to your prayer life than a foundation. But as you become accustomed to using your prayer, the newness will be tempered, and the prayer's value as the foundation of your spiritual life will become apparent. If you are beginning your prayer life with the breath prayer, regard it as the foundation upon which to build in the future.

All forms of prayer bring us more and more into an awareness of being in God's presence. Reading scripture, being faithful to morning and evening prayers, saying intercessory prayers, attending communal worship services—all are important spiritual disciplines. But each of these activities has a beginning and ending point, whereas the breath prayer is not limited to fixed times. Because it can be said anywhere at anytime, it becomes the link that holds all our activities together. Many people also find the breath prayer helpful in calming themselves so that they can give greater attention to other prayer forms. Two or three minutes of saying the breath prayer usually provides the desired sense of peace.

Why is the breath prayer so short?

The prayer is short because it flows from a basic need that one can express in a few words. Also, the brevity of the prayer makes it easy to remember and therefore suitable for people of all ages in all kinds of circumstances. Most of us find that our breath prayer takes on a rhythmic quality, and no matter what we are doing, the words that speak of our deepest need play in our mind and sing in our heart throughout the day.

How does the breath prayer differ from the mantra used in non-Christian forms of meditation?

People who receive a mantra in such practices as transcendental meditation are usually given it as part of a mystical ritual or ceremony and cautioned to limit its use. Typically those practicing this form of meditation focus on their mantra twice a day for twenty minutes.

There is nothing magical or mysterious about the breath prayer. It is not a chant or word or sound given to us by someone else. Nor does it involve secret ceremonies or rituals. Instead, it is a self-discovered prayer that arises within each of us as our personal response to God. Best of all, we can use the breath prayer anywhere at any time. Many of us find it to be the first step toward praying unceasingly.

(Questions about the Breath Prayer continues on Day 3)

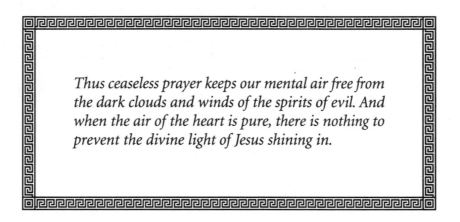

Thus ceaseless prayer keeps our mental air free from the dark clouds and winds of the spirits of evil. And when the air of the heart is pure, there is nothing to prevent the divine light of Jesus shining in.

Hesychius
fifth-century preacher and teacher
From *Writings from the Philokalia on Prayer of the Heart*

REFLECTING AND RESPONDING

In what ways do you presently pray: communal prayer in worship services, shared prayer in group study, scripture reading, hymn singing, meditation, memorized prayers, conversations with God? What prayer—or form of prayer—do you see as the foundation of your prayer life? Write this in the space provided in the drawing. In the rest of the drawing, write in what makes up your "House of Prayer." Outside the house, note prayers or ways of praying that you would like to fit in.

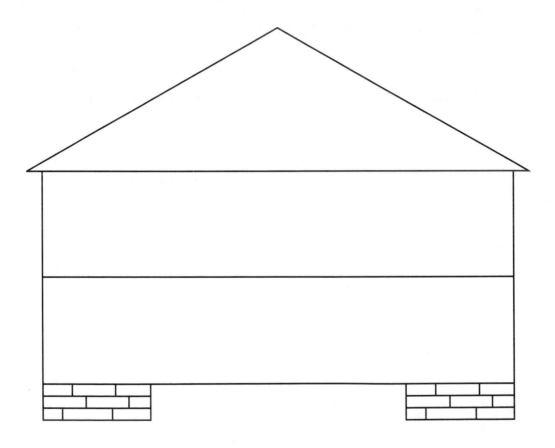

Week One, Day Three

PRAYER:

God of all creation, I give thanks that I am united in your breath
with _____ and all those joined in this journey
into prayer. May each of us become more aware of your loving
presence in our lives. Amen.

⮑ Center yourself by praying your breath prayer five times. ⮌

- After your prayer, be aware of your body. If you are tense, take several deep
  breaths to relax.

- Be aware of God's presence as you journey deeper into a life of prayer.

READING FOR TODAY:

QUESTIONS ABOUT THE BREATH PRAYER

(CONTINUED)

Is the breath prayer vain repetition?

Whenever someone asks this question, I assume the person has in mind the passage from Matthew 6:7 in which Jesus warns against insincere prayer and the mistaken belief that we will be heard for our "many words." Certainly we can say prayer with only the lips, but the personal nature of the breath prayer makes it unlikely that we will use it in a careless or vainly repetitious manner. Although the breath prayer is repeated frequently, it is not some magical way to get results from God. Rather, it acts as a focus and over time becomes as much a part of us as our own breathing.

When I was a child, my grandmother taught me that anytime I heard a siren (fire, ambulance, police) I was to pray for the people involved in the emergency. She did not stress the length of the prayer, only the need to respond in spirit to those in trouble. As an adult I have continued the practice of praying whenever I hear a siren, and many people have shared with me that they do the same. Because I have repeated this behavior for so long, it—like the breath prayer—has become second nature to me.

Does asking for a physical healing make a suitable breath prayer?

Sometimes people who are ill respond to the question "What do you want?" by saying, "I want to be healed."

I always ask, "If you were healed right now, how would you feel?"

"I'd feel peaceful," is a likely answer.

I then suggest a prayer based on that statement. Such a prayer might be"Let me feel your peace, O God." This prayer does not deny the possibility of healing but moves the focus beyond physical healing to the peace God offers, no matter what occurs.

Do people ever find two breath prayers rise within them?

Yes, people do sometimes find that two breath prayers emerge. When this happens, I suggest that they write both prayers down and ask themselves which is more personal. Which moves more deeply into their being?

Ted had discovered his prayer on a retreat. After using that prayer for several years, he called to tell me that two prayers were emerging: "Let me feel your touch, O God" (his original breath prayer) and "Lead me in your way, O God." He shared that while working in a soup kitchen once a week, he felt touched by God when he handed lunch to the people who came through the line. For Ted it was time to let go of one prayer and move into the new one. In another circumstance it could be that the person felt touched by God and, finding that a little scary, wanted to hurry up and "get on the way." In that case I would suggest the person stay with the original prayer awhile longer.

People also might have two prayers emerge when they are facing a decision or going through a trauma or short-term crisis. Over time, though, one prayer generally emerges and is used exclusively.

Will my breath prayer ever change?

Yes, your breath prayer may change. During a time of intense growth, it is not uncommon for someone's prayer to change several times. On a week-long retreat, for example, some people may change their prayer one or two times as they recognize deeper levels of need and the yearning God has for them.

For the most part, however, people tend to go through the discovery process and then keep that same breath prayer for a considerable time. If our prayer changes, it typically happens when we arrive at an insight or experience a significant life event such as marriage, death of a loved one, birth of a child, divorce, a job change, or resolution of a problem. During a time of transition we might use two prayers interchangeably. The emergence of a new prayer often occurs without our giving it any thought. One day we realize that we are saying a different prayer—a prayer that expresses our needs at a particular time in life.

Some people use a prayer for two or three years and then quickly change to two or three prayers in the course of the next year. More often than not, however, people stay with the same prayer for long periods of time—some for as long as ten and fifteen years. The important thing to remember is that each person's experience with the breath prayer is unique, and there is no norm.

One should refrain from changing the words of the prayer too often lest this frequent chopping and changing [of attention from one thing to another] should accustom the mind not to concentrate on one thing but to deviate from it and so remain for ever not firmly planted in itself; and thus it will bear no fruit, like a tree which is many times transplanted from place to place.

Callistus

fourteenth-century spiritual teacher

From *Writings from the Philokalia on Prayer of the Heart*

REFLECTING AND RESPONDING

Has your style of prayer changed over the years? On the time line, note the year of your earliest memories of prayer. From that point on, look at your life in five-year blocks of time. Write the dates and all the forms your prayer took during those periods: communal prayer, memorized prayers, personal conversations with God. It is not uncommon for some people to have periods when they did not feel they were praying at all.

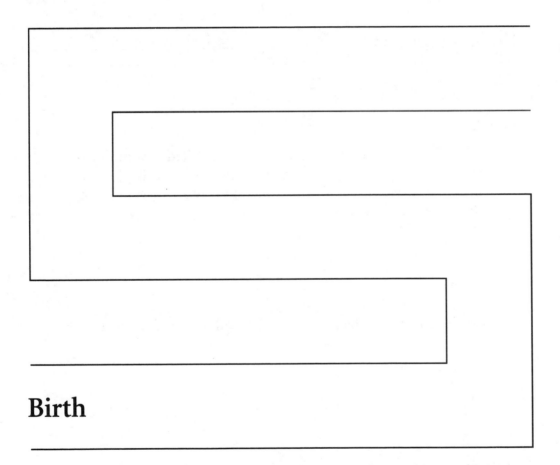

Birth

Week One, Day Four

PRAYER:

God of all creation, I give thanks that I am united in your breath with _____ and all those joined in this journey into prayer. May each of us become more aware of your loving presence in our lives. Amen.

Center yourself by praying your breath prayer five times.

- After your prayer, be aware of your body. If you are tense, take several deep breaths to relax.

- Be aware of God's presence as you journey deeper into a life of prayer.

Reading for Today:

Learning to Pray Unceasingly

Learning to pray unceasingly is like acquiring any other good habit: it takes practice. Continuing to practice until a habit becomes second nature requires discipline. For example, when we learn to knit, every stitch is painstakingly done and constantly checked to see if we are getting it right. But once we have mastered the skill, we can knit while carrying on a conversation or watching TV, seldom having to focus on the knitting.

Physical workouts such as jogging or aerobics also become second nature through practice. When we first commit to a regimen of exercise, the discipline is tedious. At times we wonder why we began. But at some point, we no longer have to give the activity our constant attention. We get to a place where we flow with the movement; our body moves with the rhythm. The inner person and the outer person are in harmony.

Likewise if prayer is to become part of our being, it requires attentiveness and discipline. Begin using your breath prayer as often as possible, saying it everywhere and under all circumstances. Say the prayer slowly, focusing on each word. The purpose is not to match the prayer to the sometimes hectic pace of your life but to bring your entire being into harmony with a calm inner self.

A good time to practice your prayer is while walking. Use half your prayer on one step and half on the other. Or walk slowly and say the whole prayer on each step. If you do some form of exercise or body movement, say the prayer in rhythm with your movement. Many people use their breath prayer while running, walking, or swimming. At first say your prayer slowly, almost gently; after a while your breath and your prayer will take on a rhythm of their own.

When you are alone, you may want to say your prayer out loud. Some people sing or chant their prayer. Changing the emphasis on the words helps the prayer become more and more your own. Many people tell me they find this change of emphasis helpful because they explore and discover various aspects and nuances of the prayer. For example:

O *God*, let me feel your love.
O God, *let* me feel your love.
O God, let *me* feel your love.
O God, let me *feel* your love.

(Learning to Pray Unceasingly continues on Day 5)

Reflecting and Responding

Pray your breath prayer in a slow, rhythmic way, emphasizing a different word each time. Repeat your prayer until you have moved through all the words at least three times.

What did you experience as you prayed?

_____

_____

_____

_____

_____

_____

Did any word(s) pop out for you? What were they? _____

_____

_____

Did a certain word take on a meaning it had not had before? What was the word and what insight did you have?

_____

_____

_____

_____

Week One, Day Five

❦

PRAYER:

God of all creation, I give thanks that I am united in your breath
with _____ and all those joined in this journey
into prayer. May each of us become more aware of your loving
presence in our lives. Amen.

↝ Center yourself by praying your breath prayer five times. ↜

- After your prayer, be aware of your body. If you are tense, take several
  deep breaths to relax.
- Be aware of God's presence as you journey deeper into a life of prayer.

READING FOR TODAY:

LEARNING TO PRAY UNCEASINGLY

(CONTINUED)

As you use your breath prayer more and more, it becomes a part of you. The process through which this happens involves the following stages:

FIRST STAGE

In the first—or oral stage—we are aware of saying the prayer, and it "resides," so to speak, in the throat and mouth. This stage is an essential part of our growth with the prayer and not vain repetition as discussed in the section "Questions about the Breath Prayer" read on Days 2 and 3. To call upon God is not vain repetition but a constant response to God's great love for us.

Learning a new way to pray requires attention and discipline. In this first stage you may find it helpful to have reminders of your commitment to the prayer.

- Many people write their prayers on note cards or labels and put them where they will see them often: the bathroom mirror, the refrigerator door, by the phone, on the dashboard. A lawyer put a small self-adhesive sticker-dot on his watch; every time he checked the time he was reminded to say his prayer.

- A teacher prays whenever the bell rings at school or the phone rings at home.

- A bank teller prays every time someone comes to his window.

- A woman whose favorite color is yellow prays whenever she sees something yellow.

- A dentist initially used her prayer each time she washed her hands at the office. Now she remembers her prayer every time she washes her hands.

- A sales rep who spends a lot of hours in his car uses his breath prayer whenever he glances in the rearview mirror.

- A doctor says the prayer each time she enters a hospital room.

Reminders to say our prayer are as personal as the prayer itself. As the prayer becomes more and more a part of us, the need to be reminded lessens.

I use my prayer in a variety of situations. If I am in traffic that tempts me to use the horn, I say my prayer instead. It has a calming effect and reminds me to respond lovingly to others. I have a dot on the frame of my computer screen, and it reminds me to be more attentive to God in the midst of my work. Sometimes I focus on the prayer for ten or fifteen seconds and feel myself move more consciously into the presence of God.

SECOND STAGE

You will be growing into this stage when the prayer moves into your mind. One day you will find yourself saying the prayer and be unaware of having said it. Or you will wake up in the morning and feel that you have been praying all night because the prayer is with you. At other times too you will find that the prayer is simply there, moving in and out of your consciousness. It might happen while you are walking or standing in line or waiting for an appointment. Then you will know that you have moved closer to unceasing prayer.

The temptation at this stage is to sit back and enjoy the experience. After all, it seems the prayer has become so much a part of you that you no longer have to consciously focus on it. Although that may seem to be the case, it is still as important to pray consciously as it was in the first stage. The goal is to have your thoughts and actions become more and more integrated.

At this stage we—and perhaps the people around us—become aware of changes in our behavior. We no longer get so upset in traffic. We are more loving. We listen intently. We feel at peace and sense that we are growing closer to God. We enjoy silence more. We can be alone without feeling lonely. Difficult tasks go more smoothly. We become aware that our prayer is influencing our entire life.

During this stage the prayer resides in our head and has begun integrating our thoughts. One young man at this stage said, "A lot of thoughts that had been troubling me are now gone because I have something else on my mind." As we use the breath prayer, the work of the Spirit continues to transform us into God's image and likeness.

(Learning to Pray Unceasingly continues on Day 6)

REFLECTING AND RESPONDING

List repetitious actions you take during a typical day:

_____   _____

_____   _____

_____   _____

_____   _____

_____   _____

What are regular occurrences in your life?

_____   _____

_____   _____

_____   _____

_____   _____

_____   _____

Draw a star by those actions and/or occurrences that could be a reminder to say your breath prayer.

Week One, Day Six

PRAYER:

> God of all creation, I give thanks that I am united in your breath
> with _____ and all those joined in this journey
> into prayer. May each of us become more aware of your loving
> presence in our lives. Amen.

Center yourself by praying your breath prayer five times.

- After your prayer, be aware of your body. If you are tense, take several deep breaths to relax.

- Be aware of God's presence as you journey deeper into a life of prayer.

READING FOR TODAY:

LEARNING TO PRAY UNCEASINGLY

(CONTINUED)

THIRD STAGE

In this stage the prayer moves into the heart. The shift comes about as we continue to pray with fervor and become more disciplined. It is as though the mind itself has moved into the heart, and a union of the two takes place. When this occurs, our awareness of peace and love increase; we think with love and make decisions based on that love. We find ourselves opening our hearts to others, recognizing both their suffering and their joy and becoming more conscious of how our prayer unites us in spirit.

FOURTH STAGE

In this last stage of the integration process, the prayer moves so totally into our lives that it spreads throughout our body. So deep is the rhythm of the breath prayer that it unites with our breathing and is truly part of our being. After having used her prayer for four years, Cecelia describes how integrated the prayer can be:

> When I am faithful with my breath prayer and I awake at night, there is a pulse, a rhythm. I am experiencing my body praying for me as I sleep. Through my breath prayer I have found a way to have a constant attitude, a way of turning to God with my mind, heart, and soul—my whole body. This way of praying has led me to experience God's love in ways I never expected. God is a God of glad surprises.

Because we are all different, the time it takes for each stage varies. For most people, the passage from stage to stage takes months, even years. So if you think your progress is slow, do not be discouraged. At whatever stage you find yourself, you can gain something valuable. Whether you are beginning and the prayer seems to reside in the mouth, or whether it has begun to be a part of your whole being, continued use of the prayer will deepen your awareness of your life in God.

Begin praying your breath prayer. Say it at an even pace over and over. At times you may feel this is a silly, even childish thing to be doing, and that you cannot say the prayer one more time. That is the point at which to say it twenty times more. Discipline yourself to go on, and the time will come when you are praying unceasingly. I invite you to join the growing number of people committed to unceasing prayer. Discover your breath prayer and practice it until it is so much a part of you that it comes as naturally as breathing. Do so and you will come to experience the breadth and depth of God's love in exciting and unexpected ways.

You must never regard any spiritual work as firmly established, and this is especially true of prayer; but always pray as if beginning for the first time. When we do a thing for the first time, we come to it fresh and with a new-born enthusiasm. If, when starting to pray, you always approach it as though you had never yet prayed properly, and only now for the first time wished to do so, you will always pray with a fresh and lively zeal. And all will go well.

Theophan the Recluse
nineteenth-century monk, bishop, and spiritual director
From *The Art of Prayer: An Orthodox Anthology*

Reflecting and Responding

Have you ever thought using the prayer was silly? When and why?

_____

_____

_____

_____

How has using your breath prayer made you more aware of God's presence?

_____

_____

_____

_____

⤳❀⤲

Preparation for the Group Meeting

Look over the readings and activities of the past week and pick out an insight or experience to share with the group. Some people are more comfortable sharing something they have written prior to the meeting. Use these lines or a separate sheet of paper to identify your insight or experience.

_____

_____

_____

Remember to bring this book to the meeting. You will need it for the opening and closing prayer, and you may want to refer to something you read or wrote during the week.

Second Group Meeting

Purpose:

To share the week's experiences and honor one another's journey in prayer.

Materials needed:

- Name tags if people are not yet acquainted
- A 3 x 5 index card for each member of the group with his or her name on it (See Step 4.)
- Watch or timer
- Bible, candle in a sturdy holder, plant or fresh flowers

Preparations:

- Arrange the seating so people can see one another easily.
- Create a focal point with the Bible, candle, and plant or flowers. Have the Bible open and the candle lit as people arrive.

Procedure:

Anyone who brought a symbol may place it on the focus table. (Invite those who brought symbols to tell the group about them during the discussion time. Others may want to describe something that is symbolic for them.)

➤ 1. Begin with prayer. Ask the group to turn to this page and together pray these lines from scripture:

> You created my inmost being
> and knit me together in my mother's womb.
> For all these mysteries—
> for the wonder of myself,
> for the wonder of your works—
> I thank you.
> God, search me and know my heart;
> probe me and know my thoughts.

> Make sure I do not follow evil ways,
> and guide me in the way of life eternal.
> Psalm 139:13-14, 23-24, PA

➤ 2. Ask the group to reflect on their experiences of the past week:

- something from the readings that was especially meaningful,

- a particular insight or discovery,

- an awareness of God's presence in their lives.

Follow with three minutes of silence. (Use a watch or timer.)

➤ 3. Invite group sharing. If no one responds, use these questions to stimulate discussion. Because different people relate to different questions, it is helpful to read them all and then wait for someone to begin. At some meetings you may spend the entire discussion time on just one question.

- What has been your experience with the breath prayer so far?

- Did you have a particular discovery or insight?

- What in the readings was especially meaningful for you?

- When were you aware of God's presence this past week?

End the discussion ten minutes before the close of the meeting. This allows time for picking new prayer companions and the closing. So as not to end the discussion abruptly say, "We have five minutes of discussion time left."

➤ 4. Pick new prayer companions. Place the 3 x 5 cards face down and mix them up. Each person draws a name; those who get their own name draw again. Remind group members to write their new prayer companion's name in their workbooks.

➤ 5. Begin the closing ritual with three minutes of silence. (Use your watch or a timer.) Suggest that people say their breath prayer silently, repeating it slowly and perhaps changing the emphasis on the words. State that in the coming week, they will be asked to pray their breath prayer for three minutes before beginning the reading for the day. After the silence, ask everyone to look around the group with an awareness of how blessed you are to be able to share your journey in prayer with one another. (Take a moment for everyone to look around.) Ask the group to turn to this page in the book. Together pray:

Thank you, God, for bringing us together
on this journey that takes
us deeper into a life of prayer.
Guide us to look within
that we might discover our deepest needs
and place them in your hands.
Grant us the grace to know
that you are with us always
and to feel your
loving presence in our lives.
Amen.

NOTES

PRAYER:

> God of all creation, I give thanks that I am united in your breath
> with _____ and all those joined in this journey
> into prayer. May each of us become more aware of your loving
> presence in our lives. Amen.

> ∾ Pray your breath prayer for three minutes. ∾
> Pray your prayer silently or aloud, or sing it to a favorite tune.

Write thoughts, feelings, or insights you had while praying or reflect on your
awareness of God's presence in your life during the past twenty-four hours.

_____

_____

_____

_____

_____

_____

READING FOR TODAY:

HISTORY OF THE BREATH PRAYER

The breath prayer is a short prayer of praise and petition that has been used since ancient times. As we breathe unceasingly, our breathing supports life and renews our corporeal system. When we use the breath prayer to develop our ability to pray unceasingly, God's love supports and renews us.

Historically, the breath prayer rose out of the Psalms. Repeated phrases from the Psalms became short prayers to remind one of the entire psalm.

Some religious traditions, have called the various forms of a breath prayer "aspiratory" or "ejaculatory" prayers. The term *aspiratory* comes from the Latin word meaning "to breathe" and *ejaculatory* from the sport of javelin throwing. Traditionally such prayers have been short and have risen from particular circumstances. In times of stress, need, or joy we may pray, "Jesus, help me" or "O God, hear my prayer" or "Praise to thee, O God." Such prayers rise spontaneously from within, sometimes flowing from us without a conscious awareness that we are praying.

It is said that Ignatius of Antioch, who was killed early in the second century because of his faith in Jesus, used a short prayer over and over while in prison. When questioned by his jailers, who thought his words were some kind of incantation, Ignatius explained that his teacher (believed to be John the Apostle) had taught him to have on his lips what was always in his heart.

Having on our lips what is always in our heart is the essence of the breath prayer, the roots of which go deep in our spiritual heritage. Within the Christian tradition of the East, we find a breath prayer called the Jesus Prayer: "Lord Jesus Christ, Son of God, have mercy on me, a sinner." The prayer grew out of a need to create a disciplined form of prayer for the thousands of monks and others seeking a deeper relationship with God. The Jesus Prayer served as a touchstone, compressing into a few words all the doctrine one needed to believe in order to be saved.

The Jesus Prayer was formulated in the sixth century and enjoyed a revival in the Christian church of the East, most notably in Greece and Russia, in the fourteenth and nineteenth centuries. *The Way of a Pilgrim*, a classic book on spirituality by an anonymous nineteenth-century peasant, describes the beauty and use of this breath prayer. Intent upon a deeper spirituality, the devout peasant visits an esteemed elder who quotes to him from sacred writings:

If, in spite of all effort, you cannot enter the interior of the heart in the way which was explained to you, then do what I will tell you and with God's help you will reach your goal. . . . While fighting distractions, diligently and continuously say, "Lord Jesus Christ, have mercy on me!" If you will persevere for some time then, without any doubt, the path to the heart will be opened to you. This has been verified through experience.

After following the elder's suggestion for some time, the pilgrim wrote,

Then I went to see the elder and told him everything in detail. He listened to me and then said, "Praise be to God that now you have both a longing for the Prayer and that the recitation of it comes easily. . . . Call on the name of Jesus all your waking moments, without counting, and humbly resign yourself to God's will expecting help from Him. I believe that He will direct your path and will not forsake you."

After receiving this direction, I spent the rest of the summer reciting the name of Jesus vocally and I enjoyed great peace. During my sleep I often dreamed that I was praying. And if I happened to meet people during the day they all seemed as close to me as if they were my kinsmen, even though I did not know them. My thoughts had quieted down completely; I thought only of the Prayer, to which my mind now began to listen, and my heart produced certain warmth and gladness.

In recent years the Jesus Prayer has again become a way of prayer for many people. Some use the traditional prayer shortened to "Lord Jesus, Son of God, have mercy on me." Others prefer, "Lord Jesus Christ, have mercy" or even the brief, "Jesus, mercy."

(History of the Breath Prayer continues on Day 2)

REFLECTING AND RESPONDING

In the reading for today, the elder tells the pilgrim on the way, "If you will persevere for some time then, without any doubt, the path to the heart will be opened to you." After a time of faithfulness to his prayer, the pilgrim enjoyed great peace. By being faithful in prayer, we too can hope to find the peace that comes when the path of the heart is opened to us.

Think of times when faithfulness to prayer brought you peace: during an illness, making a major move, preparing for holiday company, sitting in traffic. Write about one or more of your experiences:

_____

_____

_____

_____

As you think about your life right now, in what areas would faithfulness to prayer make a difference? What could you do to help yourself be more faithful in prayer?

_____

_____

_____

_____

Week Two, Day Two

❧ ✿ ❧

PRAYER:

God of all creation, I give thanks that I am united in your breath with _____ and all those joined in this journey into prayer. May each of us become more aware of your loving presence in our lives. Amen.

〜 Pray your breath prayer for three minutes. 〜
Pray your prayer silently or aloud, or sing it to a favorite tune.

Write thoughts, feelings, or insights you had while praying or reflect on your awareness of God's presence in your life during the past twenty-four hours.

_____

_____

_____

_____

_____

_____

READING FOR TODAY:

HISTORY OF THE BREATH PRAYER

(CONTINUED)

When I was a college freshman, I knew nothing of the early forms and uses of the breath prayer, but in my deeply felt desire to draw closer to God, I discovered it on my own. After studying for exams one cold December night, I decided to take a walk before going to bed. I can still recall the frostiness of the air, the sprinkling of stars in the black sky, the crunch of snow under my boots. As I walked along the nearly deserted streets of Erie, Pennsylvania, my thoughts turned to my inner spirit. I felt restless and unfulfilled. What was I seeking? Where was I going with my spiritual life?

That night I made two significant decisions: I consciously decided that I was called to be on a journey with my God and that, as a foundation of my faith life, I would use a short prayer to keep me spiritually disciplined.

In the ensuing months I made it a point to pray often. When I walked, drove, or waited in line, I said my short prayer. In much the same way that I breathed without consciously thinking about it, prayer was spontaneous within me.

Only later did I learn that I had discovered a way to pray that had been used through the centuries. But instead of using the Jesus Prayer or one of its variations, I realized that a more personal prayer had come to me. It arose from my personal need and clarified who I was. I felt then, and continue to believe, that the better we understand ourselves and our needs, the better we are able to understand our relationship with God.

Since that long ago winter night, I have instructed countless people in this personal approach to prayer. The goal has always been to help them arrive at a breath prayer that is distinctly their own—a prayer that puts on their lips what is deep in their heart. Just as breathing goes on naturally within our bodies, our personal prayer of praise and petition plays in our mind and sings in our heart even when we are not focusing on it. As we find more and more ways to use our prayer, we are sustained by the renewed awareness that we are in God's presence. I invite you to experience the many gifts and insights that come from using the breath prayer, a prayer we discover for ourselves.

When we come to any new form of prayer, it is helpful to learn from someone who has used the form for a long time. Even though we might not think we have a prayer within us, we do.

There is an often repeated story about a gentle monk who was well known for his prayer life. Someone younger came to him and asked how he had reached the point where prayer was constant.

"Looking back," said the monk, "it seems that the prayer has always been deep in my heart. Once it was like an underground spring covered over with a stone. Then one day Jesus came along and removed the stone. The spring has been bubbling ever since."

Reflecting and Responding

Today's reading states, "The better we understand ourselves and our needs, the better we are able to understand our relationship with God." We may want many things in life, but what do we truly need? Take this opportunity to look at the needs and wants in your life. Write them on the lines below.

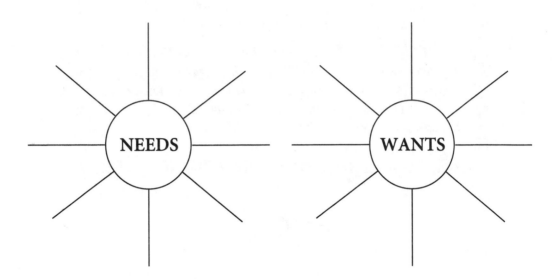

- Which do you have more of—needs or wants?
- What do you learn about yourself by looking at this completed activity?

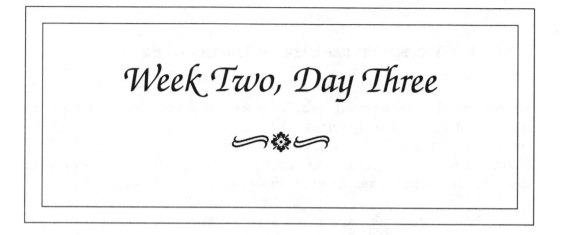

Week Two, Day Three

PRAYER:

> God of all creation, I give thanks that I am united in your breath
> with _____ and all those joined in this journey
> into prayer. May each of us become more aware of your loving
> presence in our lives. Amen.

Pray your breath prayer for three minutes.
Pray your prayer silently or aloud, or sing it to a favorite tune.

Write thoughts, feelings, or insights you had while praying or reflect on your
awareness of God's presence in your life during the past twenty-four hours.

_____

_____

_____

_____

_____

_____

READING FOR TODAY:

THE SCRIPTURAL BASE FOR UNCEASING PRAYER

For prayerful people, scripture is the living word that provides signposts along the path of their spiritual journey. The call to be people of prayer is woven through both the Hebrew and Christian scriptures. In this passage from the Hebrew Scriptures, Moses beseeches the people of Israel never to forget the deeds of Yahweh and to make this remembrance part of their daily lives:

> Listen, Israel: Yahweh our God is the one Yahweh. You shall love Yahweh your God with all your heart, with all your soul, with all your strength. Let these words I urge on you today be written on your heart. You shall repeat them to your children and say them over to them whether at rest in your house or walking abroad, at your lying down or at your rising; you shall fasten them on your hand as a sign and on your forehead as a circlet; you shall write them on the doorposts of your house and on your gates.
>
> Deuteronomy 6:4-9, JB

Like our faith ancestors, we too need reminders of God's action in our lives. The letters of the Christian scripture admonish us to keep ourselves mindful of God through unceasing prayer.

In the letter to the Hebrews (13:15–16) we read:

> Through him, then, let us continually offer a sacrifice of praise to God, that is, the fruit of lips that confess his name. Do not neglect to do good and to share what you have, for such sacrifices are pleasing to God.

To the Thessalonians (1 Thessalonians 5:16-18), the apostle Paul wrote, "Rejoice always, pray without ceasing, give thanks in all circumstances."

Colossians 4:2 tells us, "Devote yourselves to prayer, keeping alert in it with thanksgiving."

No matter what the circumstances of our lives, our call is to respond with prayer. Romans 12:12 counsels, "Rejoice in hope, be patient in suffering, persevere in prayer."

Ephesians 6:18 states, "Pray in the Spirit at all times in every prayer and supplication."

To pray without ceasing on every possible occasion means that *we are to be in a state of remembrance of what God has done and is doing for us.* We are to praise God and to ask for what we need. When we do this, our prayer is one of praise and petition.

(The Scriptural Base for Unceasing Prayer continues on Day 4)

REFLECTING AND RESPONDING

In today's reading, the quote from Deuteronomy tells us that the Hebrews kept themselves mindful of God's law by wearing headbands or arm bands and by hanging reminders on the gates and doorposts of their homes. They did this so that the law to love God might be written on their hearts. What items do you have in your home, car, or workplace that serve as reminders of this law to love God? (For example: pictures, plaques, books, art objects)

_____

_____

_____

Do you wear or keep on your person anything that reminds you of God's abiding presence in your life? (For example: angel pin, cross, ring)

_____

_____

If you do not have any such reminder of God, have you considered getting something? What might it be?

_____

Some things may not be intrinsically religious, yet they speak to us of God: a sunrise or sunset, a flower, a child's drawing, a gift from a friend. What calls God to mind for you?

_____

_____

_____

_____

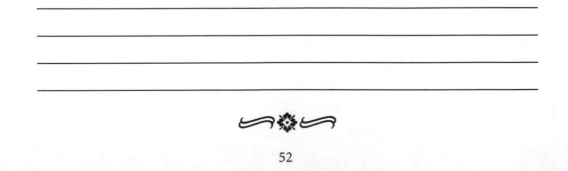

Week Two, Day Four

PRAYER:

> God of all creation, I give thanks that I am united in your breath
> with _____ and all those joined in this journey
> into prayer. May each of us become more aware of your loving
> presence in our lives. Amen.

⤳ Pray your breath prayer for three minutes. ⤳
Pray your prayer silently or aloud, or sing it to a favorite tune.

Write thoughts, feelings, or insights you had while praying or reflect on your
awareness of God's presence in your life during the past twenty-four hours.

_____

_____

_____

_____

_____

READING FOR TODAY:

THE SCRIPTURAL BASE FOR UNCEASING PRAYER

(CONTINUED)

In addition to praying unceasingly, scripture tells us to pray in the Spirit, which is understood more fully by examining the Hebrew word *ruach*. It is a word that we can translate as "wind," "breath," or "spirit." The spirit, or *ruach* of God, is breathed into all living beings.

Time and again throughout scripture, we see God breathing life into creation. In Ezekiel 37:9 we read,

> Then he said to me, "Prophesy to the breath, prophesy, mortal, and say to the breath: Thus says the Lord God: Come from the four winds, O breath, and breathe upon these slain, that they may live."

Likewise in John 20:22 we find reference to the Spirit's being breathed upon the disciples: "When he had said this, he breathed on them and said to them, 'Receive the Holy Spirit.'"

Genesis 1:1-2 speaks of God's spirit being imparted in the wind:

> In the beginning when God created the heavens and the earth, the earth was a formless void and darkness covered the face of the deep, while a wind from God swept over the face of the waters.

In John 3:8, we again see God's spirit as wind: "The wind blows where it chooses, and you hear the sound of it, but you do not know where it comes from or where it goes. So it is with everyone who is born of the Spirit."

The scriptures also speak of God's spirit entering into us. In the Hebrew Scriptures, God says through the prophet Ezekiel (36:27), "I will put my spirit within you, and make you follow my statutes and be careful to observe my ordinances."

Paul, in a letter to the Galatians (4:6), writes, "And because you are children, God has sent the Spirit of his Son into our hearts, crying, "Abba! Father!"

Through prayer we feel a oneness with God. When we cannot pray for ourselves, the Spirit speaks for us:

Likewise the Spirit helps us in our weakness; for we do not know how to pray as we ought, but that very Spirit intercedes with sighs too deep for words. And God, who searches the heart, knows what is in the mind of the Spirit, because the Spirit intercedes for the saints according to the will of God.

Romans 8:26-27

What a comfort to know that the Spirit intercedes for us in times when we are too filled with doubt or sorrow or anger to reach out to God on our own. But aside from those times, how do we take responsibility for our prayer lives? How do we remain constant in prayer? When our schedules are already overcrowded, how can we possibly praise and thank God unceasingly? An answer lies in the breath prayer—a prayer that enables us to pray without ceasing and keeps us mindful that we share the breath of God.

> *Thus ceaseless prayer keeps our mental air free from the dark clouds and winds of the spirits of evil. And when the air of the heart is pure, there is nothing to prevent the Divine light of Jesus shining in.*

Hesychius
fifth-century preacher and teacher
From *Writings from the Philokalia on Prayer of the Heart*

REFLECTING AND RESPONDING

As people of prayer, we invite the Spirit into our lives. When that happens we cannot stop praying, for the Spirit prays without ceasing. Write a prayer of thanksgiving for God's gift of the Holy Spirit. If there was a time in your life when you could not pray for yourself and you felt the Spirit interceding for you, incorporate that into your prayer.

Week Two, Day Five

PRAYER:

> God of all creation, I give thanks that I am united in your breath
> with _____ and all those joined in this journey
> into prayer. May each of us become more aware of your loving
> presence in our lives. Amen.

> ∽ Pray your breath prayer for three minutes. ∽
> Pray your prayer silently or aloud, or sing it to a favorite tune.

Write thoughts, feelings, or insights you had while praying or reflect on your
awareness of God's presence in your life during the past twenty-four hours.

_____

_____

_____

_____

_____

_____

READING FOR TODAY:

CALLED TO BE PRAYERFUL

Most of us who come from a Christian background have said prayers, read prayers, listened to prayers, and memorized prayers. We speak of mental prayer, of prayerful meditation, of reciting prayers, of studying prayers. But how often are we challenged to *become* prayer? How often are we so God-centered that we become other-centered and think of prayer as a gift of ourselves to another person?

The gift of ourselves varies with the circumstances. In one situation, the gift might be a listening ear or a helping hand; in another, a warm embrace, a bit of our time, a word of encouragement or comfort or cheer. The gift of ourselves is almost certain to involve us in social justice issues—in clothing the naked, feeding the hungry, giving drink to the thirsty, finding shelter for the homeless. This other-centeredness is what the apostle Paul refers to when he writes, "it is no longer I who live, but it is Christ who lives in me" (Galatians 2:20).

So far you may feel that you fall far short of this ideal. Do not be discouraged. When looking in a mirror, few of us see a saint reflected back. We are all at different places on our spiritual journey, but wherever we are, even one small step forward makes the goal less distant. When we focus on the present—on where we live and love and interact with others—opportunities to become prayer are all around us.

Prayer involves us in seeking, growing, loving. In our desire to draw closer to God, there is a danger we will wear ourselves out with a multitude of prayers that become routine or even meaningless. This is most likely to happen when prayer comes from the mind alone. But when prayer is integrated into our whole being, we become aware of what prayer can do for us and for our relationship with God.

A truly prayerful person lives more and more in an attitude of prayer—more and more turned toward God. Such a person does not constantly beseech God but is instead attentive to the life of the Spirit and able to hear: "Be still, and know that I am God" (Psalm 46:10). Through attentive stillness, we are better able to concentrate on where we are on our spiritual journey and where God is calling us.

Scripture tells us, "Be perfect, therefore, as your heavenly Father is perfect" (Matthew 5:48). You may respond, *Be perfect as God is perfect! Isn't that asking just too much?* Indeed, it is. Expecting perfection from ourselves and others leads to numerous problems. We can avoid many of these problems by understanding the intent of the passage. In the scriptural context, the word *perfect* means "whole" or "integrated" or "together." God does not call us to be perfect in the commonly understood use of the word but rather to be whole, fully integrated people with body, mind, and spirit in harmony. When we function as a whole, we are in communion with life; we are able to see, hear, and respond with a full and joyous heart.

(Called to Be Prayerful continues on Day 6)

REFLECTING AND RESPONDING

Today's reading challenges us to go beyond being prayerful people and to become prayer. We do this through the gift of self. Turning life into prayer takes time, desire, and sustained effort. But when we make that effort, life becomes richer and more satisfying. What opportunities do you have for giving of yourself and becoming prayer? Remember that the giving can be as simple as a friendly greeting or as demanding as taking over for a caregiver who needs a day off.

Opportunities I have for giving the gift of self:

Home:_____

_____

Work: _____

_____

Community:_____

_____

Church:_____

_____

Other: _____

_____

In the coming week I resolve to give this gift of self:

_____

_____

Week Two, Day Six

PRAYER:

> God of all creation, I give thanks that I am united in your breath
> with _____ and all those joined in this journey
> into prayer. May each of us become more aware of your loving
> presence in our lives. Amen.

Pray your breath prayer for three minutes.
Pray your prayer silently or aloud, or sing it to a favorite tune.

Write thoughts, feelings, or insights you had while praying or reflect on your
awareness of God's presence in your life during the past twenty-four hours.

_____

_____

_____

_____

_____

_____

Reading for Today:

Called to Be Prayerful

(continued)

Prayer is a search for meaning, and through prayer we try to discover God's will for our lives. Many people view God's will as something chipped in stone at the time of their birth. They then spend a lifetime trying to determine what God has in mind for them. Much of the frustration of this quest is eliminated if we understand what is meant by God's will.

The word *will*, which we translate from the Latin *voluntas*, means "yearning" in both Hebrew and Greek. So the question "What is God's will for me?" is more precisely "What is God's yearning for me?" Yearning describes the longing that two people in love have for each other; not a yearning of the mind alone or of the heart alone but of the *whole being*. When someone yearns for us, it awakens our yearning, which in turn intensifies the yearning of the other until we come together in some way. Thus God's yearning is not something we find outside ourselves, but rather something we become aware of and experience from within. In trying to determine whether our yearning is a response to God's yearning for us, we might ask ourselves these questions:

- Will following my yearning make me more loving?

- Will I be a better servant of my gifts?

- Will I feel more fulfilled?

- Will I have a greater sense of inner peace?

When we can answer yes to these questions, we know that our yearning and God's yearning for us are one and the same.

The breath prayer keeps us attentive to God. This attentiveness leads to a greater sense of God's presence in our lives and of where we are being called. We are then no longer simply prayerful people but are on our way to becoming prayer.

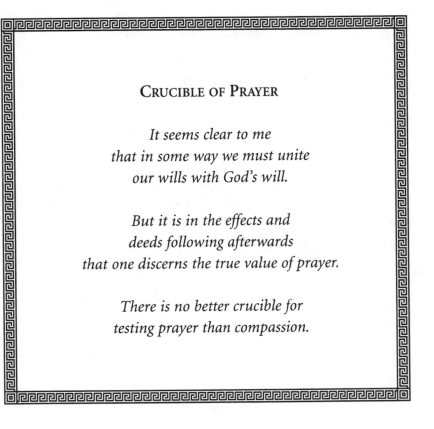

CRUCIBLE OF PRAYER

It seems clear to me
that in some way we must unite
our wills with God's will.

But it is in the effects and
deeds following afterwards
that one discerns the true value of prayer.

There is no better crucible for
testing prayer than compassion.

Teresa of Avila (1515–82)
Spanish mystic and writer
From *Meditations with Teresa of Avila*

Reflecting and Responding

Look into your heart and determine your deepest yearning. Write it here:

_____

To determine if your yearning is a response to God's yearning for you, go back to the four questions in today's reading. Your answers will help you know if your yearning is in harmony with God's yearning for you.

What do you plan to do to satisfy your yearning?

_____

_____

_____

Preparation for the Group Meeting

Look over your reflections on your prayer and the readings and activities of the past week. Pick out an insight or experience to share. Some people are more comfortable sharing something they have written prior to the meeting. Use these lines or a separate sheet of paper to identify your insight or experience.

_____

_____

_____

Remember to bring this book to the meeting. You will need it for the opening and closing prayer, and you may want to refer to something you read or wrote during the week.

THIRD GROUP MEETING

PURPOSE:

To share experiences of the past week and honor one another's journey in prayer.

MATERIALS NEEDED:

- Name tags if people are not yet acquainted

- A 3 x 5 index card for each member of the group with his or her name on it (See Step 4.)

- Watch or timer

- Bible, candle in a sturdy holder, plant or fresh flowers

PREPARATIONS:

- Arrange the seating so people can see one another easily.
- Create a focal point with the Bible, candle, and plant or flowers. Have the Bible open and the candle lit as people arrive.

PROCEDURE:

Anyone who brought a symbol may place it on the focus table. (Invite those who brought symbols to tell about them during the discussion time. Others may wish to describe something that is symbolic for them.)

➤ 1. Begin with prayer. Ask the group to turn to this page and together pray these lines from scripture:

> I rejoice in the way of your decrees
> with joy above all wealth.
> I will meditate on your precepts
> and concentrate on your ways.

> I will delight in your statutes
> and never forget your words.
> Be good to your servant
> that I may live to keep your words.
> Open my eyes that I may marvel
> at the wonders of your law.
> I am a pilgrim on earth.
> Show me your commands.
> My soul is consumed with longing
> for your decrees at all times.
> Psalm 119:14-20, PA

➤ 2. Ask group members to reflect on their experiences of the past week:

- something from the readings that was especially meaningful,

- a particular insight or discovery,

- an awareness of God's presence in their lives.

Follow with three minutes of silence. (Use a watch or timer.)

➤ 3. Invite group sharing. If no one responds, use these questions to stimulate discussion. Because different people relate to different questions, read them all and then wait for someone to begin. At some meetings, you may spend the entire discussion time on just one question.

- What has been your experience with the breath prayer so far?

- Did you have a particular insight or discovery this week?

- What in the readings was especially meaningful for you?

- When were you aware of God's presence this past week?

(End the discussion ten minutes before the close of the meeting. This allows time for picking new prayer companions and the closing ritual. So as not to end the discussion abruptly say, "We have five minutes of discussion time left.")

➤ 4. Pick new prayer companions. Place the 3 x 5 cards face down and mix them up. Each person draws a name; those who get their own name draw again. Remind group members to write their new prayer companion's name in their workbooks.

➤ 5. Begin the closing ritual with three minutes of silence. (Use your watch or a timer.) Suggest that everyone silently say his or her breath prayer, repeating it slowly and perhaps changing the emphasis on the words. To be in silent prayer with others can be a powerful experience. After the silence, ask everyone to look around the group with an awareness of how blessed you are to be able to share your journey in prayer with one another. (Take a moment for everyone to look around.) Ask the group to turn to this page in their books. Together pray,

Thank you, God, for bringing us together
on this journey that takes
us deeper into a life of prayer.
Guide us to look within
that we might discover our deepest needs
and place them in your hands.
Grant us the grace to know
that you are with us always
and to feel your
loving presence in our lives.
Amen.

NOTES

Week Three, Day One

֍

PRAYER:

> God of all creation, I give thanks that I am united in your breath
> with _____ and all those joined in this journey
> into prayer. May each of us become more aware of your loving
> presence in our lives. Amen.

⌒ Pray your breath prayer for three minutes. ⌒
Pray your prayer silently or aloud, or sing it to a favorite tune.

Write thoughts, feelings, or insights you had while praying or reflect on your
awareness of God's presence in your life during the past twenty-four hours.

_____

_____

_____

_____

_____

_____

READING FOR TODAY:

THE BREATH PRAYER BRINGS CHANGE

Steven was a young husband, father, and dentist with a flourishing practice who sought a spiritual center in his life. "Can it really be true that God hears my breath prayer?" he asked. "Or am I praying just for me? It's hard for me to believe that it's possible to know—I mean really know—God. If only there were some magic words that would make this happen."

Having discovered his breath prayer, Steven found it difficult to get into the discipline of using it. This led him to question everything related to his spiritual life. He did not yet understand that to wonder in the depths of ourselves is the beginning of a great journey. Questioning is something we all go through on our way to a deeper spirituality.

Like Steven, we too may wish for something to put us in union with God instantly. This desire is understandable since we live in a society that emphasizes immediate gratification and instant results. Even though we are conditioned to believe that change occurs quickly, that is seldom the case. Instead, God prepares the soil in which our spirituality takes root and then tends us with loving care. But we also have a part to play. We need to make a conscious effort to continue to grow. One of the ways to do this is through use of the breath prayer. Attentiveness to prayer increases our awareness of the presence of God in our lives. This awareness leads us to be more insightful about ourselves and our relationship with God. But instead of happening in a flash, change and growth come about gradually.

The change required of us calls to mind the scripture, "Again I tell you, it is easier for a camel to go through the eye of a needle than for someone who is rich to enter the kingdom of God" (Matthew 19:24). Some scripture scholars believe that the eye of a needle in this passage refers to one of the narrow gates of Jerusalem. Before a camel could go through, the driver had to remove all that the camel carried. Only when the camel was unburdened could it pass through that gate into Jerusalem.

We all carry baggage that encumbers our lives—possessions, relationships, ambitions, hurtful feelings, memories of past failures. Some attachments are necessary and good, but a red flag goes up when we are attached compulsively to any of them. In one case a woman was so attached to her car that she asked to be buried in it. In another case, a son assaulted his parents because he felt smothered by their love. Even though these attachments are extreme, they motivate us to look at our own lives and see what we need to change to bring us into better balance. And unlike the camel that had to take up its burden again after passing through the gate, we have the option of remaining unburdened.

Robert's use of the breath prayer led him to an awareness that he needed to unburden his life. At age thirty-three, he was a pastor in a church that had just completed a building program. He had spent so much time on the program that he was out of touch with his prayer life. This is how he expressed himself in a journal entry:

> *I need to reorder some aspects of my life. I need to stop buying things and get out of debt. I need to start seeing Jesus in everyone. I need to care for my body and get going on some exercise. I need to bridle my anger. I'm becoming aware that it's like getting rid of a stubborn stain: each time I wash it, it gets lighter and lighter, but then I find another stain somewhere else.*

Rose was a widow of means who could satisfy all of her material needs and most of her wants. In a journal entry, she recorded what happened after she settled into regular use of the breath prayer:

> *I was finding little things I could do without, and it made it so practical because they were things I'd been wanting to cut out for a long time, but the discipline of the breath prayer and my growing awareness of God's caring for me are making it easier.*

At first we may be reluctant to unpack our camel, but when we do we discover that we are carrying things we do not even want. This can be likened to moving. The beginning stage of any move is seeing what possessions we can discard—things we will not need where we are going. Getting down to those things in life that are really important underlies the entire process of change.

(The Breath Prayer Brings Change continues on Day 2)

REFLECTING AND RESPONDING

Today's reading points up the need to unburden ourselves of whatever encumbers our lives and hinders our spiritual growth.

What baggage can you get rid of as you unpack your camel? Be as specific as possible. In the interest of privacy you may in some instances want to use initials, abbreviations, or your own shorthand.

Possessions: _____

_____

Relationships: _____

_____

Resentments: _____

_____

Hurtful memories: _____

_____

Past failures: _____

_____

Other: _____

_____

Week Three, Day Two

PRAYER:

God of all creation, I give thanks that I am united in your breath
with _____ and all those joined in this journey
into prayer. May each of us become more aware of your loving
presence in our lives. Amen.

~ Pray your breath prayer for three minutes. ~
Pray your prayer silently or aloud, or sing it to a favorite tune.

Write thoughts, feelings, or insights you had while praying or reflect on your
awareness of God's presence in your life during the past twenty-four hours.

_____

_____

_____

_____

_____

_____

READING FOR TODAY:

THE BREATH PRAYER BRINGS CHANGE

(CONTINUED)

The more we recognize our compulsive attachments, the more we see ourselves as we really are. Seeing ourselves as we are leads to a growth in humility. Sometimes humility has been considered self-deprecating—a matter of putting ourselves down—when, in fact, this is not the case at all. To be humble is to recognize the truth about who we are before God and others. This involves recognizing our strengths as well as our weaknesses.

For a long time I was unable to accept a compliment. If someone said, "That's a beautiful shirt," I invariably responded by saying that it was old or that it was just something I picked up on sale. If someone told me my teaching was great, I laughed (a good defense, of course) and said, "Oh, I bet you say that to all your teachers." I was never able to say a simple thank-you and leave it at that. But then an incident occurred that gave me a lesson in humility—a lesson from which I benefited greatly.

At the time I was in Cleveland, Ohio, and had given what I believed to be an especially good presentation one Saturday evening. Afterward a young woman who introduced herself as Mary came up to me. She had a warm smile and in a forthright manner said, "Ron, that was the most beautiful talk I ever heard. You moved something within me."

I laughed self-consciously and really did mean it when I said, "Oh, yes, the spirit of God does wonders."

Instantly Mary's friendliness turned to anger. "That's the whole trouble with you Christians!" she yelled. "Can't you ever take responsibility for anything? You always think you're so special that you have to proclaim the Spirit is with you. Are you afraid we won't see it?"

Mary forced me to see that instead of being humble, I unwittingly made myself special by *not* accepting her compliment. What she needed from me was a simple thank-you; saying that would have ministered to her. But instead of focusing on her, I immediately turned the attention back to myself. The experience with Mary illustrated that when we walk in the Spirit, we do not need to proclaim it in loud words. It is evident by the way we live our lives.

False humility prompted me to respond to Mary in a way that was less than honest. Honesty is perhaps the greatest gift we can bring to our relationships. And often being honest means saying no. I spent many years saying yes when I wanted to say no and then complaining about what I had agreed to do. My work suffered, and I realized that instead of being in control of situations, I had let situations control me. Gradually I came to understand that I seldom said no because I didn't want to admit there were things I did not want to do or did not do well. Also, saying yes was a subtle way to get people to notice me and love me.

(The Breath Prayer Brings Change continues on Day 3)

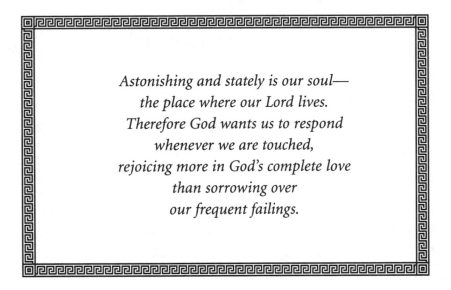

Astonishing and stately is our soul—
the place where our Lord lives.
Therefore God wants us to respond
whenever we are touched,
rejoicing more in God's complete love
than sorrowing over
our frequent failings.

Julian of Norwich (1342–1416/1423)
English mystic
From *Meditations with Julian of Norwich*

REFLECTING AND RESPONDING

Seeing ourselves as we are is an important first step in personal growth. That means looking not just at our weaknesses but also at our strengths. Once we admit our weaknesses, we can do what is necessary to change. Traits in myself that I see as weaknesses: _____

_____

By acknowledging our strengths, we know what we have to build on.

Let the checklist remind you of your positive traits and help you determine areas where you need to be more attentive.

	Sometimes	Most of the Time	Almost Never
Truthful	_____	_____	_____
Trustworthy	_____	_____	_____
Friendly	_____	_____	_____
Kind	_____	_____	_____
Faithful	_____	_____	_____
Courteous	_____	_____	_____
Patient	_____	_____	_____
Understanding	_____	_____	_____
Keep a confidence	_____	_____	_____
Sense of humor	_____	_____	_____
Fair-minded	_____	_____	_____
Humble	_____	_____	_____
Forgiving	_____	_____	_____
Loving	_____	_____	_____
Responsible	_____	_____	_____
Compassionate	_____	_____	_____
	_____	_____	_____
	_____	_____	_____

Week Three, Day Three

PRAYER:

> God of all creation, I give thanks that I am united in your breath
> with _____ and all those joined in this journey
> into prayer. May each of us become more aware of your loving
> presence in our lives. Amen.

Pray your breath prayer for three minutes.
Pray your prayer silently or aloud, or sing it to a favorite tune.

Write thoughts, feelings, or insights you had while praying or reflect on your
awareness of God's presence in your life during the past twenty-four hours.

_____

_____

_____

_____

_____

_____

READING FOR TODAY:

THE BREATH PRAYER BRINGS CHANGE

(CONTINUED)

Most people would agree that saying no is difficult. But doing so is critical if we are to have the time needed to replenish ourselves spiritually. Even Jesus said no to demands placed on him when he needed to go away by himself.

Tom, a husband and father of three teenagers, began using the breath prayer and realized that he had to say no to some of his activities in the community if he wanted to restructure his life. In his journal he tells how using the breath prayer brought him to this realization:

> *Before, I was so busy doing all the good things that I had really forgotten to leave time to pray. I was using every second to plan my life and what I would do next. Now, using the breath prayer, I spend much more time being aware of living in God's presence, which I always was. I was just not as aware as I could be.*

When we become aware of living in God's presence, we also develop the sense that *where we are is where we are supposed to be.* For many people this is a liberating idea. Our society tells us that we have to get through one thing in order to get on with something else. Thus, it is difficult for us to comprehend that with God *there is no place to get to; there is only a life to live.*

Too often people feel that spiritual growth is a job that needs doing and that to earn God's love they have to work harder and harder. I believe this thinking is faulty on both counts: God's love is not something we have to earn, and in the spiritual life the premise that more is better is replaced by the idea that simpler is better. That is not to say we cannot lead involved and busy lives, but at the center of our being we need a single-minded focus on God. The breath prayer helps us maintain that focus and keeps us living in the present instead of looking back at the past or ahead to the future.

After using the breath prayer for a number of years, Jean, a mother of two small children who was involved in many causes, shared how she grew to value the here and now:

My life relationships have become much smoother as a result of my efforts. I became more in tune with myself, my body, my work. I have become more loving and tolerant of people. I see them as having a beauty of their own. I live only periodically in that loved space, and I have not given myself completely to God's love, but more and more each day I feel a letting go. I am between two worlds—desiring not to go back and yet unable to jump into the future. I am striving perhaps too hard for that total change, but I know that where I am now is where I am supposed to be. God loves me in the here and now. That is my place to love.

As we move more and more into the presence of God, we cannot remain the same. God's loving action transforms us and we, in turn, become more loving toward those with whom we live and work and play. But for most of us, change comes slowly—so slowly sometimes that we wonder if it is happening at all. During those times, we must be patient and continue praying. Change is occurring within us, and in due time we will experience the graces of remaining faithful to our prayers.

*The fruit
and the purpose
of prayer
is
to be one with
and like
God
in all things.*

Julian of Norwich (1342–1416/1423)
English mystic
From *Meditations with Julian of Norwich*

REFLECTING AND RESPONDING

Today's reading reminds us that in our life with God *there is no place to get to; there is only a life to live.* Another way of saying this is "grow where you're planted." Think of three specific actions you can take in the coming week to grow right where you are. Depending upon your situation, these can be anything from enjoying time with your family to volunteering in a shelter for the homeless. Write what you plan to do on the lines inside the flowers.

GROWING WHERE I AM

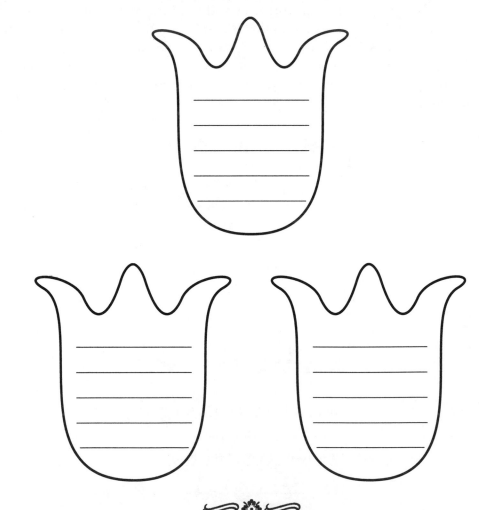

Week Three, Day Four

PRAYER:

God of all creation, I give thanks that I am united in your breath
with _____ and all those joined in this journey
into prayer. May each of us become more aware of your loving
presence in our lives. Amen.

    Pray your breath prayer for three minutes.
Pray your prayer silently or aloud, or sing it to a favorite tune.

Write thoughts, feelings, or insights you had while praying or reflect on your
awareness of God's presence in your life during the past twenty-four hours.

_____

_____

_____

_____

_____

_____

Reading for today:

A Turning Point

Many people who use the breath prayer and become more aware of God's presence experience what has been called "the gift of tears." This gift is more than crying. The gift of tears is an experience of being overwhelmed by a sense of oneself in relationship to God. In this intimate and awesome state, we find ourselves crying, and there seems to be no way to stop the flow of tears. Our awareness of how much we are loved by God just as we are, without judgment, fills us to overflowing with gratitude.

Scripture tells us that on one occasion, a woman went to a house where Jesus had been invited for dinner, and while there, experienced the gift of tears:

> And a woman in the city, who was a sinner, having learned that he [Jesus] was eating in the Pharisee's house, brought an alabaster jar of ointment. She stood behind him at his feet, weeping, and began to bathe his feet with her tears and to dry them with her hair. Then she continued kissing his feet and anointing them with the ointment
>
> Luke 7:37-38

Tears might also come when we see more clearly how we have denied our love and turned away from God. Such was the experience of the disciple Peter:

> But Peter said, "Man, I do not know what you are talking about!" At that moment, while he was still speaking, the cock crowed. The Lord turned and looked at Peter. Then Peter remembered the word of the Lord, how he had said to him, "Before the cock crows today, you will deny me three times." And he went out and wept bitterly
>
> Luke 22:60-62

Most of the time the gift of tears is like a cloudburst; the floodgates open and we cry as if there is no stopping. In this entry from my own journal, I describe the experience I shared earlier about talking with one of my graduate school professors:

> *When you suggested we pray together and said, "As our Savior Christ has taught us we are bold to say," I could feel a lump forming*

in my throat and I didn't know whether or not I'd be able to pray. I blurted, "Our Father" and then was overwhelmed with tears.

Martha, a grade-school teacher who drove back and forth to work, made this journal entry about her gift of tears:

> *I don't know what was happening, but I was just sitting in the car at the intersection waiting for the light to change and saying the prayer. All of a sudden I started to cry. I was so aware of how much God loved me. It only lasted a moment, but it seemed like I'd broken through into a new place.*

The gift of tears is a turning point in people's lives—a time of going deeper into the life of the Spirit. The apostle Paul talks about this in one of his letters:

> You were taught to put away your former way of life, your old self . . . and to be renewed in the spirit of your minds, and to clothe yourselves with the new self, created according to the likeness of God in true righteousness and holiness.

> Ephesians 4:22-24

In scripture and throughout our history as Christians, the gift of tears has marked spiritual turning points. Sometimes when we "lose control" and cry, we try to ignore what has happened or make light of it. But there is no denying what has taken place. James, a businessman in his early thirties, had just finished reading the above quote from Ephesians when he experienced the gift of tears. He described what happened in this journal entry:

> *I then felt the beginning—the beginning of the new me, the beginning of the touch of the love of God. I felt appreciation, gratitude, and love. I then walked out into the rain, humble, and felt the rain and the cleansing comfort. There were small instances when my old Me came out and said, "This is foolish; this event is silly," but those feelings didn't stay very long because the old Me didn't have any lasting power.*

Through the gift of tears, the power of living in the presence of God becomes more dynamic. We have a sense of mission or ministry or caring for others. We also have a renewed interest in loving and a more intense desire for prayer. It is as though we have been pushed from one dimension to another where we sense a new light and new possibilities for living.

It is not uncommon that after experiencing the gift of tears, our breath prayer changes. Edward was a seminary student whose prayer was "Jesus, let me walk with you." One afternoon at a retreat on spirituality he asked to talk with me. The two of us went for a walk around a nearby lake, and Edward began to unravel his concerns about his family. He talked especially about the hostility he felt toward certain family members. As we walked along the path, Edward stopped suddenly. He seemed transformed as he looked at me and said, "You know, *Jesus is walking with us right now.*"

"Yes, he is," I responded.

At that moment, Edward's eyes were opened and—like the apostle Paul— scales of darkness that had held back insights into his life fell away. The spirit of truth made Edward free. Pieces of his life and the mosaic of his relationship with God and his family came into focus. We continued our walk in prayer as Edward's tears flowed.

Later that evening a downcast Edward came to me. "I just can't say my prayer anymore," he said. "Asking Jesus to let me walk with him no longer fits." But even as Edward spoke, a knowing look came over his face. With awe in his voice, he said, "Maybe that's because I already have walked with Jesus. When you and I were going around the lake, I experienced walking with him!"

I suggested to Edward that the time had come for him to sit in silence and another prayer would be known to him. At this point in his life he would have another answer to God's question, "Edward, what do you want?"

Edward's acceptance of the gift of tears made him a good deal more conscious of God's presence in his life, and he was moved to serve others in greater love. Perhaps you too will experience the gift of tears on your journey to a deeper understanding of God's love. If so, regard the experience as a blessing and know that it is a sign of growth in the Spirit.

REFLECTING AND RESPONDING

We all have turning points in our lives—times when circumstances or a particular decision takes us in a certain direction. Sometimes a turning point is evident in our actions; other times it is internalized and forever changes the way we view life or God or a particular relationship.

Look back at your life and determine the major turning points. Starting with the earliest one you can remember, note them here:

_____

_____

_____

_____

_____

_____

_____

_____

_____

_____

Did the direction you chose take you toward God? away from God? made no difference that you are aware of?

If the gift of tears accompanied any of your turning points, place an asterisk beside it.

⌒❀⌒

Week Three, Day Five

PRAYER:

> God of all creation, I give thanks that I am united in your breath
> with _____ and all those joined in this journey
> into prayer. May each of us become more aware of your loving
> presence in our lives. Amen.

> Pray your breath prayer for three minutes.
> Pray your prayer silently or aloud, or sing it to a favorite tune.

Write thoughts, feelings, or insights you had while praying or reflect on your
awareness of God's presence in your life during the past twenty-four hours.

_____

_____

_____

_____

_____

_____

Reading for today:

The Breath Prayer Becomes Part of Life

Some beautiful new houses were built at the end of the street where we once lived. But standing as they did in the middle of their lots surrounded only by dirt, they didn't fit in with the setting. Although the houses were complete in themselves, they stood apart from one another, giving the neighborhood a disjointed look. Then one morning a truck from the local nursery arrived, and landscapers went to work. Within days they had laid all the sod and planted shrubbery. What a change! Now greenery joined the new houses with the others on the block, and suddenly the neighborhood looked unified.

The breath prayer serves much the same purpose as the greenery around those houses in that it unites and unifies all our ways of praying. No single form of prayer is weakened, changed, or neglected. Instead, each is enhanced because the breath prayer brings a new depth and dimension to familiar ways of praying.

As we practice praying unceasingly, we become more and more conscious of living in God's presence. We have a better grasp of what it is to be a child of God, as expressed in this scripture:

> For all who are led by the Spirit of God are children of God. For you did not receive a spirit of slavery to fall back into fear, but you have received a spirit of adoption. When we cry, "Abba! Father!" it is that very Spirit bearing witness with our spirit that we are children of God, and if children, then heirs, heirs of God and joint heirs with Christ—if, in fact, we suffer with him so that we may also be glorified with him.
>
> Romans 8:14-17

As children of God, we increasingly walk in the light. Therefore we have less to fear because scripture assures us that even in the dark, we have the light that is Jesus to follow: "What has come into being in him was life, and the life was the light of all people. The light shines in the darkness, and the darkness did not overcome it" (John 1:3-5).

Unceasing prayer keeps us mindful that we are children of God, and as such we walk in a light that will see us through any difficulty. But making prayer as much a part of our lives as breathing requires discipline. Friends with whom I have talked about spiritual direction kid me because of the many times I say, "Discipline is the key."

Sometimes prayer comes with ease. It is not hard to pray when we feel moved by the Spirit or when we find ourselves in desperate situations. Neither is it hard to pray when we are in a good mood and things are going well or when we are with people who pray as we do. But we are called to do more than pray when prayer comes easily; we are called to become prayerful people—to be people who pray always in the Spirit, in the breath of God. The more aware we are of our call to be people of prayer, the greater our awareness that our breath and the breath of God are becoming one.

The only way to find out how placing yourself in God's presence will affect your life is to try it. When you feel an urge to make an unkind remark, silently say your breath prayer. When you feel a need to top someone's story, say your prayer. When you find yourself getting angry, say your prayer. Pray when waiting at a stoplight or for an appointment. Pray while hugging the children or teaching a class. Center on your breath prayer while you do the dishes or paint the house. Turn off the radio when you drive and say your breath prayer. Instead of watching TV after dinner, go for a walk and pray. Over time you will discover that by praying more and more unceasingly you feel an overflow of love—a love that goes out to others. This ceaseless praying becomes a deep form of intercessory prayer.

Many of us spend most of our time with others. Because we are seldom alone, we are like a pendulum stuck to one side, out of balance. As the breath prayer becomes more a part of you, do not be surprised if you want to spend more time alone or feel a need for a few minutes of silence each day. To rebalance your schedule, enter silence and pray. For some people this is a foreign experience; that is how accustomed we have become to relentless activity.

As you use your breath prayer, your pace tends to slow and you feel a greater integration of mind, body, and spirit. You are more in tune with your work. You begin freeing yourself from compulsive attachments, whether behaviors, possessions, or people. You become more honest about your abilities and your life. You are more patient and will likely find your horizons widening or shifting.

(The Breath Prayer Becomes Part of Life continues on Day 6)

The principal thing is to stand with the mind in the heart before God, and to go on standing before Him unceasingly day and night, until the end of life.

Theophan the Recluse
nineteenth-century monk, bishop, and spiritual director
From *The Art of Prayer: An Orthodox Anthology*

REFLECTING AND RESPONDING

Think back to yesterday. When did you pray and what form did your prayer take?

Morning:

_____

_____

_____

_____

Afternoon:

_____

_____

_____

_____

Evening:

_____

_____

_____

_____

Reflect on how the breath prayer fits in with your other forms of prayer.

Week Three, Day Six

꙳❀꙳

PRAYER:

> God of all creation, I give thanks that I am united in your breath
> with _____ and all those joined in this journey
> into prayer. May each of us become more aware of your loving
> presence in our lives. Amen.

꙳ Pray your breath prayer for three minutes. ꙳
Pray your prayer silently or aloud, or sing it to a favorite tune.

Write thoughts, feelings, or insights you had while praying or reflect on your
awareness of God's presence in your life during the past twenty-four hours.

_____

_____

_____

_____

_____

_____

READING FOR TODAY:

THE BREATH PRAYER BECOMES A PART OF LIFE

(CONTINUED)

We all have a horizon upon which we base our actions. It is the familiar base from which we operate. As long as that horizon, or base, is there—and we see it—we have our bearings and go on with life. After important life events such as a marriage, a death, a birth, the loss of a job, a graduation, a birthday marking a new decade, or a significant insight, we need to reestablish our horizon.

As we use the breath prayer, old horizons widen or shift and new possibilities appear. Having someone with whom to share our spiritual growth helps us see and explore the possibilities. We grow not as individuals alone but as individuals within a community. Even though we may feel we pray alone, our prayer unites us with all who pray and are attentive to God's presence. The more attentive we are to God, the more attentive and caring we become to others as well. Prayer brings us into a fullness with God, which motivates us to work for social justice and to take a stand against oppression in its various forms.

Ken was an insurance salesman who had been using his prayer for about two years when he said to me, "I'm feeling that it's not right for me to just pray daily. I've got to do something." What Ken did was work with the homeless in his community. He later told me that he found great value and a deep sense of touching God through his work in an overnight shelter. "I use my breath prayer as I say good night to the people," he said. "It reminds me that I'm in God's presence."

Any teacher in the area of spirituality, or friend knowledgeable about the subject, will assure you that your present horizon is what it should be for where you are right now. At the same time that teacher or friend will encourage you to move on. If you do not have someone with whom to share, look for such a person. Consider the counselors, ministers, or leaders you know, and see if you are drawn to one of them.

While in *The Breath of Life* program, you have had people with whom to share your spiritual journey. When the program concludes, you may want to join or start a prayer group in which members pray for one another and discuss what is happening in their spiritual lives.

The breath prayer gives us common ground on the journey of the Spirit. Even though we have our own prayer, we know that others with their own prayer also pray unceasingly. When I go into a group and recognize someone who I know uses a breath prayer, I find it a warming experience.

In a neighborhood where we once lived, the post office was notorious for its long lines at the lunch hour. (If I overuse the idea of praying while in line, it is because of my numerous experiences of doing so at this post office!) As I waited one day, I glanced at another line and noticed Barbara, a young woman who had attended one of my classes on the breath prayer. Our eyes met, and with a smile she said, "I know what you're doing, and I bet you know what I'm doing." We both laughed and continued waiting in line, in prayer.

The breath prayer enables us to be prayerful in the ordinary activities of life. By using the breath prayer as much as possible at all times and in all places, we soon realize what an enriching, vital part of our life it has become.

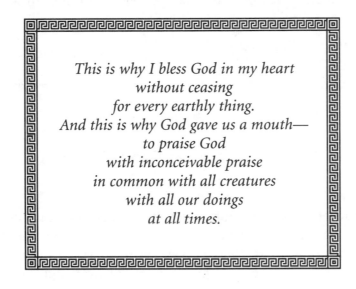

This is why I bless God in my heart
without ceasing
for every earthly thing.
And this is why God gave us a mouth—
to praise God
with inconceivable praise
in common with all creatures
with all our doings
at all times.

Mechtild of Magdeburg (c. 1209–c.1283)
German mystical writer
From *Meditations with Mechtild of Magdeburg*

REFLECTING AND RESPONDING

Today's reading states, *The more attentive we are to God, the more attentive and caring we become to others as well.* The breath prayer helps us be attentive to God. Since discovering your prayer, do you find that you are more attentive and caring to others? If yes, in what way(s)?

_____

_____

If you have found the breath prayer helpful, could one of your caring actions be teaching it to someone else? Because the prayer is short and can be said so easily, the elderly, the ill, or anyone in a stressful circumstance may find it especially useful. For many people, the breath prayer is a wonderful way to express joy and praise.

I could teach the breath prayer to:

_____

PREPARATION FOR THE GROUP MEETING

Look over your reflections on your prayer and the readings and activities of the past week. Pick out an insight or experience to share. Some people are more comfortable sharing something they have written prior to the meeting. Use these lines or a separate sheet of paper to identify your insight or experience.

_____

_____

_____

Remember to bring this book to the meeting. You will need it for the opening and closing prayer, and you may want to refer to something you read or wrote during the week.

FOURTH GROUP MEETING

PURPOSE:

To share experiences of the past week and honor one another's journey in prayer.

MATERIALS NEEDED:

- A 3 x 5 index card for each member of the group with his or her name on it (See Step 4.)
- Watch or timer
- Bible, candle in a sturdy holder, plant or fresh flower

PREPARATIONS:

- Arrange the seating so people can see one another easily.
- Create a focal point with the Bible, candle and plant or flowers. Have the Bible open and the candle lit as people arrive.

PROCEDURE:

Anyone who brought a symbol may place it on the focus table. (Invite those who brought symbols to tell about them during the discussion time. Others may wish to describe something that is symbolic for them.)

➤ 1. Begin with prayer. Ask the group to turn to this page and together pray these lines from scripture:

> You, Yahweh, are all I have,
> and you give me all I need:
> my life is in your hands.
> How wonderful are your gifts to me;
> how good they are!

> I praise Yahweh, who guides me,
> and in the night my conscience teaches me.
> I am always aware of your presence;
> you are near, and nothing can shake me.
> And so I am full of happiness and joy,
> and I always feel secure.

> You will show me the path that leads to life;
> your presence fills me with joy,
> and your help brings pleasure forever.
> Psalm 16:5-9, 11, PA

➤ 2. Ask the group to reflect on their experiences of the past week:

- something from the readings that was especially meaningful,

- a particular insight or discovery,

- an awareness of God's presence in their lives.

Follow with three minutes of silence. (Use a watch or timer)

➤ 3. Invite group sharing. If no one responds, use these questions to stimulate discussion. Because different people relate to different questions, it's helpful to read them all and then wait for someone to begin. At some meetings the entire time for discussion may be spent on just one question.

- What has been your experience with the breath prayer so far?

- Did you have a particular insight or discovery?

- What in the readings was especially meaningful for you?

- When were you aware of God's presence this past week?

End the discussion ten minutes before the close of the meeting. This allows time for picking new prayer companions and the closing ritual. So as not to end the discussion abruptly say, "We have five minutes of discussion time left."

➤ 4. Pick new prayer companions. Place the 3 x 5 cards face down and mix them up. Each person draws a name; those who get their own name draw again. Remind group members to write their new prayer companion's name in their workbooks.

➤ 5. Begin the closing ritual with three minutes of silence. (Use your watch or a timer.) Suggest that people silently say their breath prayer, repeating it slowly and perhaps changing the emphasis on the words. After the silence, ask everyone to look around the group with an awareness of how blessed you are to be able to share your journey in prayer with one another. (Take a moment for everyone to look around.) Ask the group to turn to this page in their books. Together pray:

> Thank you, God, for bringing us together
> on this journey that takes
> us deeper into a life of prayer.
> Guide us to look within
> that we might discover our deepest needs
> and place them in your hands.
> Grant us the grace to know
> that you are with us always
> and to feel your
> loving presence in our lives.
> Amen.

NOTES

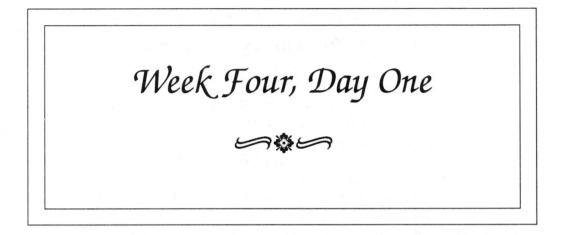

Week Four, Day One

PRAYER:

God of all creation, I give thanks that I am united in your breath
with _____ and all those joined in this journey
into prayer. May each of us become more aware of your loving
presence in our lives. Amen.

~ Pray your breath prayer for three minutes. ~
Pray your prayer silently or aloud, or sing it to a favorite tune.

Write thoughts, feelings, or insights you had while praying or reflect on your
awareness of God's presence in your life during the past twenty-four hours.

_____

_____

_____

_____

_____

_____

READING FOR TODAY:

A SPECIAL TIME AND PLACE FOR PRAYER

In addition to praying while doing whatever it is we do, we may also feel a need for a special time and place for prayer. *The length of time we take to be in prayer is not as important as the fact that we take the time.* What I suggest is called "sitting prayer," because that is exactly what we do—we sit in a more intense time of being aware of the presence of God.

If you have never sat in prayer, start modestly—perhaps for only five minutes. If you are accustomed to sitting in silence, try ten. The idea is not to let yourself be ruled by a specified time but to tailor the time to you and your spiritual needs. When we are excited about starting something new, it is tempting to set a lengthy time. But it is better to do five minutes regularly than twenty minutes today, five tomorrow, and ten the day after.

The key to success in sitting prayer is discipline. Some days you will look forward to the sitting-prayer time, and on others you will wonder why you cannot sit still. In this sense, prayer is like training for the race that the apostle Paul speaks about:

> Do you not know that in a race the runners all compete, but only one receives the prize? Run in such a way that you may win it. Athletes exercise self-control in all things; they do it to receive a perishable wreath, but we an imperishable one.
> 1 Corinthians 9:24-25

You will need a schedule and the inner discipline to adhere to it. Here is where sharing with a friend or a group can be a great help. Do your sitting prayer in a place where you feel "at home" in prayer. This might simply be a corner of a room where you have a picture, a Bible, a candle, or something else that makes the space special to you. If you are fortunate enough to have an unused room or one that is seldom used, make that your place of prayer. For seating, it is preferable to use a straight-backed chair or to sit on the floor on a cushion.

People intent on sitting in prayer become creative about finding space. One woman cleaned out a closet and then put her Bible and a favorite picture on the shelves. When it is time for her sitting prayer, she opens the closet door, moves a chair in front of the closet, and has her special place.

A professional man does his sitting prayer when he arrives at his office. He opens his closet door and sits quietly in front of a picture of Jesus he has hung on the inside of the door.

Many people create their special place at a dining room table. Each time they sit down to pray, they open their Bible and light a candle.

(A Special Time and Place for Prayer continues on Day 2)

REFLECTING AND RESPONDING

Do you feel a need to have a special time and place for prayer? Where could you create such a place?

_____

_____

_____

What could you include in that special place?

_____

_____

_____

When could you sit in prayer?

_____

_____

_____

If you are not already sitting in prayer, what do you think the benefits of it might be for you?

_____

_____

_____

Week Four, Day Two

PRAYER:

God of all creation, I give thanks that I am united in your breath with _____ and all those joined in this journey into prayer. May each of us become more aware of your loving presence in our lives. Amen.

Pray your breath prayer for three minutes.
Pray your prayer silently or aloud, or sing it to a favorite tune.

Write thoughts, feelings, or insights you had while praying or reflect on your awareness of God's presence in your life during the past twenty-four hours.

_____

_____

_____

_____

_____

_____

READING FOR TODAY:

A SPECIAL TIME AND PLACE FOR PRAYER

(CONTINUED)

Ritual is important, and I suggest that it be part of your time spent in prayer. When getting ready to do anything special, we usually go through a ritual: we get dressed up for a night out, we have birthday and anniversary rituals, we even make special preparations before sitting down to watch a ball game or a long movie on TV. The following ritual helps us become more aware that our sitting prayer is a special time spent in God's presence.

STEP ONE

Wash your hands. The hand washing serves as a reminder of a passage through water, which scripture views as a transition into a new way of life or ministry to others. We see this in both the Hebrew and Christian scriptures:

> I will take you from the nations, and gather you from all the countries, and bring you into your own land. I will sprinkle clean water upon you, and you shall be clean from all your un-cleannesses, and from all your idols I will cleanse you.
>
> Ezekiel 36:24-25

> And when Jesus had been baptized, just as he came up from the water, suddenly the heavens were opened to him and he saw the Spirit of God descending like a dove and alighting on him. And a voice from heaven said, "This is my Son, the Beloved, with whom I am well pleased."
>
> Matthew 3:16-17

STEP TWO

Set a timer for the length of time you plan to be in prayer. (This makes it unnecessary for you to look at a watch or clock.) Some days five minutes will seem like one minute. Other days you will think you have prayed for half an hour, when in fact it has been only four minutes! A timer allows you to peacefully focus on prayer in the knowledge that when the time is up, a bell or buzzer will let you know.

STEP THREE

Read a verse from scripture as a reminder that we are fed from the constancy of God's word. Read only a line or a verse. I recommend the Psalms or John's Gospel because one can find a meaningful line or verse readily. The intent is not to ponder the scripture but to place ourselves more intently in the presence of God.

STEP FOUR

Sit in prayer. Slowly and rhythmically repeat your breath prayer. If random thoughts enter your mind, be assured that this is natural. As you become aware of the thoughts, calmly bring your focus back to the breath prayer. Writers in the early centuries of the church noted that the prayer brought calm attentiveness. In our stillness we can be attentive.

Some people find it helpful to begin their sitting time by saying the breath prayer aloud, then saying it ever more softly until they become increasingly silent within themselves. Remember that the nuance of the prayer can change depending upon the words we emphasize: *God,* let me feel your peace. God, *let* me feel your peace. Changing the emphasis of the words can help keep us attentive.

Morning is best for most people to sit in prayer only because the discipline is then taken care of and does not get pushed aside by other matters. One caution about praying in the morning, however, is that we may get caught up in what I call the "gas station mentality" of spirituality. I think especially of Bill, whose job required that he fly around the country. "My life just seems like I'm going eighty [miles per hour] all the time," he said. "If I don't get some prayer time in the morning, I get to the end of the day and it's as if I haven't thought of God at all. I've got to gas up in the morning so I can make it through the day."

Prayer is not something we do just to gas up. It is a way of life. Having a special place and time for prayer is good and spiritually rewarding, but our prayer for the day does not begin and end there. The important thing is that we are attentive to God's presence throughout the day, and the breath prayer enables us to do that.

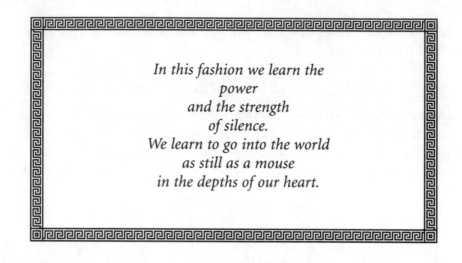

*In this fashion we learn the
power
and the strength
of silence.
We learn to go into the world
as still as a mouse
in the depths of our heart.*

Mechtild of Magdeburg (c. 1209–c.1283)
German mystical writer
From *Meditations with Mechtild of Magdeburg*

Reflecting and Responding

Consider a typical day's schedule and decide on the best time to sit in prayer. Then commit yourself to doing it daily. If you cannot fit daily prayer into your schedule, try to sit three or four times a week.

I will commit myself to sit in prayer at this time:

Monday: _____

Tuesday: _____

Wednesday: _____

Thursday: _____

Friday: _____

Saturday: _____

Sunday: _____

Week Four, Day Three

PRAYER:

God of all creation, I give thanks that I am united in your breath with _____ and all those joined in this journey into prayer. May each of us become more aware of your loving presence in our lives. Amen.

⤳ Pray your breath prayer for three minutes. ⤳
Pray your prayer silently or aloud, or sing it to a favorite tune.

Write thoughts, feelings, or insights you had while praying or reflect on your awareness of God's presence in your life during the past twenty-four hours.

_____

_____

_____

_____

_____

_____

READING FOR TODAY:

A JOURNAL FOR REFLECTION

One of the best ways to reflect on your prayer is to keep a journal. After each time of sitting prayer, take three to five minutes to write in a notebook what you have experienced. *This is not meant to be a tedious task.* Simply write the date, the time of day, and at least two sentences about what happened during your prayer. You might note the thoughts you had, experiences you recalled, emotions you felt, or physical reactions. Journal entries reveal changes in the mind and heart much the way a family photo album shows physical changes.

Journals can be any size or kind. Some people prefer a size that fits in the pocket or purse. Others like to use notebook paper and keep the pages in a binder. Still others—myself included—do their journaling on a computer.

The following journal entries reveal the kinds of things people write. The entries were made during the first weeks of using the breath prayer. Rebecca, a retired government employee, did her journaling on the veranda of her Florida home:

> *This journal kept getting in my way. Will I remember what to write down? All the outside sounds kept coming in—do the birds always chirp so loudly in the A.M.? Does the dog always breathe so heavily? A few really quiet seconds of a peaceful feeling. And wonder of wonders, was ten minutes really so short?*

A mother of two teenage daughters and very involved in church work, Mary Ellen reveals how her prayer time created an oasis of calm in a busy life:

> *I am very quiet. Even to write seems an effort. I write slowly. Fifteen minutes seemed to have passed pleasantly and quickly. I was reluctant to stop. After perhaps five minutes I became very still, began to pray silently instead of out loud. My mind kept up an observing commentary, but the stillness surrounded all. The phone rang, and I knew I would not rise from my prayer to answer it.*

Peter was a retired business executive whose mind was always so busy that it was difficult for him to become still:

> *Felt very calm and peaceful. Found that my mind was wandering or blank, so I went back to the prayer. Felt calmer and more relaxed. My mind did not seem to wander as much.*

An anesthesiologist and single father with teenage children, Jack reveals how he began to find his spiritual center through prayer:

> *I became aware as I sat in prayer that I've known for some time that the power moving me in the direction I have been going the past four or more years was more powerful than I am. The Spirit that is moving me will not let me stop. The pages will continue to be turned, and the traveler will go on by whatever mode of transportation.*

Stephanie was a single woman in her late twenties with stylish clothes, a nice car, and everything going her way:

> *Saying "Jesus, let me hear your voice." What am I asking? Am I ready to hear him? Ready to do whatever he asks of me? This is rather frightening. I know myself so well—will it be something I can't give up? I am weighing the questions.*

The key to keeping a journal of your sitting-prayer time is keeping it simple. The surest way to do this is to limit your writing time. If you are already keeping a journal, incorporate your sitting-prayer reflections in it but key them in some way so they are easy to find when you want to refer to them in the future.

(A Journal for Reflection continues on Day 4)

REFLECTING AND RESPONDING

Starting with Week 2, Day 1, you have journaled after your three minutes of prayer. In addition to this journaling, you may already be keeping a journal. If so, making entries after your time of sitting prayer will add a new dimension to what you are already doing.

If you are new to journaling, you can take this opportunity to discover its many benefits. A professional woman in her fifties said, "After journaling for three months I can honestly say it's one of the best things I've ever done for myself. The greatest benefit is that I don't keep secrets from myself anymore."

When we are honest with ourselves, we are better able to be honest with God. What better way to grow in the life of the Spirit.

FOR THOSE ALREADY KEEPING A JOURNAL

Decide how you will incorporate your sitting-prayer reflections into your journal. Code them for easy reference: use a different color ink, put the entries on a separate page, use a heading—perhaps a symbol, word, or number.

This is how I will code my journal entries after sitting in prayer:

_____

_____

FOR THOSE NEW TO JOURNALING

Decide on the size and kind of journal that will be best for you: notebook that fits in pocket or purse, pages kept in a binder, bound book with blank pages, or on a computer. Have needed supplies available the first time you do your sitting prayer. Supplies I will need: _____

_____

Week Four, Day Four

PRAYER:

> God of all creation, I give thanks that I am united in your breath
> with _____ and all those joined in this journey
> into prayer. May each of us become more aware of your loving
> presence in our lives. Amen.

⮌ Pray your breath prayer for three minutes. ⮎
Pray your prayer silently or aloud, or sing it to a favorite tune.

Write thoughts, feelings, or insights you had while praying or reflect on your
awareness of God's presence in your life during the past twenty-four hours.

_____

_____

_____

_____

_____

_____

READING FOR TODAY:

A JOURNAL FOR REFLECTION

(CONTINUED)

Although writing is the most common way of keeping a journal, drawing, sketching, painting, and collage making are other ways. Visual journaling in which people use something other than words to express themselves is gaining in popularity. This kind of journaling does not require artistic skill. The purpose of keeping any journal is to express yourself in a way that has meaning for you. Visual journaling might be anything from an intricately drawn picture to a collage of pictures cut from magazines to a page filled with nothing more than squiggly lines.

At a retreat I was giving, Laura confided that she was having difficulty clarifying the issues she faced. She tried writing in her journal but didn't find that to be very satisfactory. "Have you ever drawn anything . . . done any sketching?" I asked.

Laura said she enjoyed sketching, so I suggested she keep a visual journal during her retreat. After each of her meditations she drew a picture that captured her experience. At the beginning of the retreat one of her drawings was of a big circle squished sideways. "I just felt like everything was closing in on me," she explained. At the end of the week, Laura showed me her sketch of the sun rising over a mountain scene. "I feel like the sun is just coming up in my life," she said.

Whatever form your journal takes, it is for your eyes only—unless, of course, you choose to share it. All that matters is that it be an outlet for honest self-expression and have meaning for you.

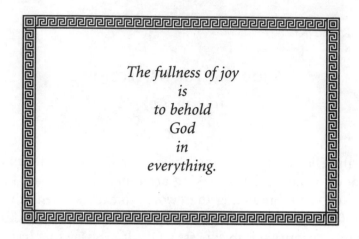

The fullness of joy
is
to behold
God
in
everything.

Julian of Norwich (1342–1416/1423)
English mystic
From *Meditations with Julian of Norwich*

REFLECTING AND RESPONDING

If you have not tried visual journaling, let this exercise be your introduction. If you already journaled in this way, you are familiar with the surprising and often illuminating images that appear on your paper. Read the following psalm. After you have finished—or even as you read—sketch what comes to mind. Sketch on this page or on one of the Notes pages in this workbook.

How dear to me is your dwelling, O Lord of hosts!
My soul has a desire and longing for the courts of the Lord;
my heart and my flesh rejoice in the living God.

The sparrow has found her a house
and the swallow a nest where she may lay her young;
by the side of your altars, O Lord of hosts,
my King and my God.

Happy are they who dwell in your house!
they will always be praising you.
Happy are the people whose strength is in you!
whose hearts are set on the pilgrims' way.
Psalm 84:1-4, *Book of Common Prayer*, 1979

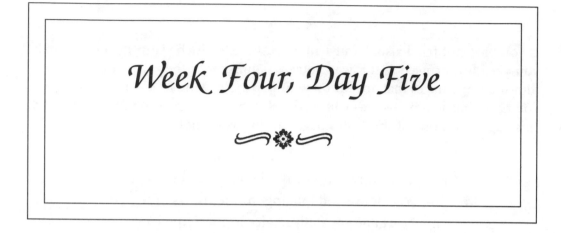

Week Four, Day Five

PRAYER:

God of all creation, I give thanks that I am united in your breath with _____ and all those joined in this journey into prayer. May each of us become more aware of your loving presence in our lives. Amen.

↬ Pray your breath prayer for three minutes. ↫
Pray your prayer silently or aloud, or sing it to a favorite tune.

Write thoughts, feelings, or insights you had while praying or reflect on your awareness of God's presence in your life during the past twenty-four hours.

_____

_____

_____

_____

_____

_____

READING FOR TODAY:

WHAT CAN YOU HOPE TO EXPERIENCE?

I asked some people who have used the breath prayer over a period of time if they would share their experiences. They agreed in the hope that their sharing would encourage others to discover their breath prayer and find a new closeness with God.

Mary is a psychotherapist with grown children who has been using her breath prayer for thirteen years. She says that although there have been on and off times of being faithful to the prayer, she lives most of her daily life being attentive to God's presence. She still loves to dance when she prays, just as she did when she made this journal entry years ago:

> *I've been using the breath prayer for a little longer than a year now, and I think the most important thing I've come to see is how closely my body is connected to my prayer. When I first began to use the prayer, I was tense and full of aches and pains when I did the sitting. Just sitting still was hard for me. I was always running. But I am continuing to slow down, to feel better and to be more aware of how important it is for me to be aware that my body is a gift from God.*

Shawn, a psychologist who deals mainly with patients in crisis situations, tells how he uses his prayer in his work:

> *I am a counselor, and after using the breath prayer for over two years, I find that I am able to use it in my practice more and more. I look at my clients and pray for them. I find I am more insightful and rely more on the promptings within me in my work. I know I am more loving.*

Marie is an actress in community theater whose journal entry reveals her poetic side:

I was forged in the fiery furnace, melted down in the flames of pain and lost in agony and fear and knowledge of my nothingness till all that was left was a spark, a tiny cinder. God breathed life on that spark till it became an eternal flame and I was born.

John sought spiritual direction during a midlife crisis and made this entry:

One great truth that has overwhelmed me is that while we can approach God as a loving Father, he is still sovereign over all. It is with awe and trembling that we receive this privilege. It was not cheap grace but a profound awareness of a level of existence more profound and powerful and bold than one could in human thought imagine.

Richard is a young pastor just starting his ministry in a large suburban parish:

Leading the congregation in worship has changed for me since I have been using the breath prayer. I find myself praying during the silent periods. I find that I am more centered and at peace when I celebrate the worship.

When Theresa reached her mid-twenties, she began dealing with issues related to her rejection as a child:

There has been much pain in seeing myself as I really was, but there has also been much joy. I feel most that I wish I had more people to share this great joy with.

Sam is an engineer, who in his middle years was searching for meaning in his life:

My life with God has been transformed. Praying unceasingly has led me into a state I never thought possible. To be in the presence of God and to be aware of that is a great gift. Praise be to God.

Ted, a clergyman in his late thirties, has used the breath prayer over a period of years and shared his experiences with it in a newsletter to his congregation:

"How would you respond if Jesus were to walk into the room and say, 'Ted, what do you want?'" That question was put to me ten years ago by Ron DelBene. . . .

The word "joy" immediately came to my mind. So I prayed, "Father, let me feel your joy." I taped this prayer inside my desk drawer. I wrote it in my calendar. I found ways to remind myself to pray this prayer many times each day. It became a "breath prayer" that I prayed for eight months.

Over time, the prayer was answered. It was time for a new prayer focus. While showering one morning at a weekend retreat, . . . I prayed, "Father, radiate your love through me." The new prayer had a dual focus: to receive God's love through and through, and to be a vessel for sharing God's love. I prayed this prayer from October 1981 until May 1991.

In May, I was at a camp for a five-day session on spiritual formation. After a lecture we were asked to spend an hour reflecting on John 15. I sat in the chapel looking at a picture of Jesus. The word "abide" from John 15 converged with the large, inviting hand of Jesus in the picture to prompt another breath prayer: "Jesus, abide in me." For five months, this was my prayer. A breath prayer often leads one to other prayer concerns. A breath prayer can also lead one to another breath prayer. So, after five months, I began to note in my journal a shift in the prayer.

Now, I'm praying, "Jesus, keep me simple." Prayer, like compound interest for an investor, is cumulative. Simple people have joy. Love radiates through simple people. The spirit of Christ abides in simple Christians. This particular prayer may be the focus of my praying for a few months or ten years or eternity. I'll always remember that it was born in anticipation of Advent. "Jesus, keep me simple," is my way of preparing for Christmas this year.

Each of these breath prayers has been a gift from God. It's not just something my brain has generated. I receive these prayers as a gift to offer back to God in gratitude for the purpose of my transformation.

Just as each of us is unique, so too is our prayer life. No two people will experience the breath prayer in exactly the same way. What we all have in common, however, is the same God—the God who moves within and among us and unites us in the life of the Spirit. Through use of the breath prayer we grow in the Spirit and become more and more conscious of God's everlasting love and presence in our lives.

Often, though, we feel unworthy of God's love. And in a certain sense we are. After all, who are you and who am I? Among so many, we are as tiny grains of sand upon the beach. Yet we have each been called and called right where we are—weak, not yet perfect, sometimes seeing ourselves as unlovable. But that is the great mystery of God who has chosen to love us where we are, as we are.

REFLECTING AND RESPONDING

In today's reading several people share their experience of using the breath prayer. What has been your experience? Was your prayer immediately apparent or did it take you a while to discover it ? What do you use as reminders to say your prayer? Has using your prayer been helpful to you? Why or why not? In the space below, write about your experience with the breath prayer in one of the following ways:

- respond to any or all of the above questions

- note changes in your life since you began using your prayer

- describe your experience with the breath prayer as though you were writing to a friend

_____

_____

_____

_____

_____

_____

_____

_____

_____

_____

_____

_____

_____

Week Four, Day Six

PRAYER:

God of all creation, I give thanks that I am united in your breath with _____ and all those joined in this journey into prayer. May each of us become more aware of your loving presence in our lives. Amen.

⤳ Pray your breath prayer for three minutes. ⤳
Pray your prayer silently or aloud, or sing it to a favorite tune.

Write thoughts, feelings, or insights you had while praying or reflect on your awareness of God's presence in your life during the past twenty-four hours.

_____

_____

_____

_____

_____

_____

READING FOR TODAY:

Yesterday's reading finished the text of *The Breath of Life: A Simple Way to Pray* from which this workbook was developed. Several of the quotations about prayer and the spiritual life included in the book have been incorporated into this workbook. The reading for today consists of two final quotations that speak to the life of the spirit and the journey that takes us closer to God.

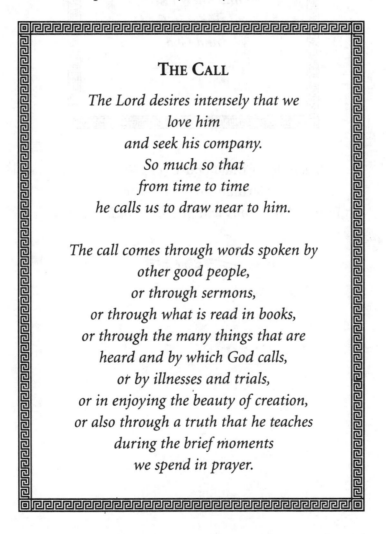

THE CALL

The Lord desires intensely that we
love him
and seek his company.
So much so that
from time to time
he calls us to draw near to him.

The call comes through words spoken by
other good people,
or through sermons,
or through what is read in books,
or through the many things that are
heard and by which God calls,
or by illnesses and trials,
or in enjoying the beauty of creation,
or also through a truth that he teaches
during the brief moments
we spend in prayer.

Teresa of Avila (1515–82)
Spanish mystic and writer
From *Meditations with Teresa of Avila*

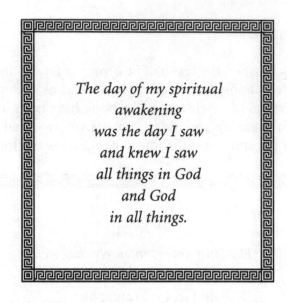

The day of my spiritual
awakening
was the day I saw
and knew I saw
all things in God
and God
in all things.

Mechtild of Magdeburg (c. 1209–c.1283)
German mystical writer
From *Meditations with Mechtild of Magdeburg*

Reflecting and Responding

Reflect on the quotations in today's reading. Underline or circle words, phrases, and images that speak to you in a special way. In the space below make your own statement about what living in the Spirit means to you. Sign and date what you write.

_____

_____

_____

_____

_____

Preparation for the Group Meeting

Look over your reflections on your prayer and the readings and activities of the past week. Pick out an insight or experience to share. Some people are more comfortable sharing something they have written prior to the meeting. Use these lines or a separate sheet of paper to identify your insight or experience.

_____

_____

_____

Remember to bring this book to the meeting. You will need it for the opening and closing prayer, and you may want to refer to something you read or wrote during the week.

NOTES

FIFTH GROUP MEETING

PURPOSE:

To share experiences and celebrate being part of *The Breath of Life* program.

MATERIALS NEEDED:

- Watch or timer
- Bible, candle in a sturdy holder, plant or fresh flowers
- Anything that would help celebrate the end of the program

PREPARATIONS:

- Arrange the seating so people can see one another easily.
- Create a focal point with the Bible, candle, and plant or flowers. Plants and flowers symbolize growth and change that has occurred during the program. Have the Bible open and the candle lit as people arrive.

PROCEDURE:

Anyone who brought a symbol may place it on the focus table. (Invite those who brought symbols to tell about them during the discussion time. Others may wish to describe something that is symbolic for them.)

➤ 1. Begin with prayer. Ask the group to turn to this page and together pray these lines from scripture:

> Yahweh, you are my shepherd;
> I shall not want.
> In verdant pastures you give me repose.
> Beside restful waters you lead me;
> you refresh my soul.

You guide me in right paths
for your name's sake.
Even though I walk in the dark valley
I fear no evil;
for you are at my side.
Your rod and your staff give me courage.
You spread the table before me
in the sight of my foes.
You anoint my head with oil;
my cup brims over.
Only goodness and kindness follow me
all the days of my life;
and I shall dwell in your house
for years to come.
Psalm 23, PA

➤ 2. Ask group members to reflect on their experiences of the past week:

- something from the readings that was especially meaningful,

- a particular insight or discovery,

- an awareness of God's presence in their lives.

Follow with three minutes of silence. (Use a watch or timer.)

➤ 3. Invite group sharing. Because this is the last meeting, shorten the usual discussion time by half to allow time to reflect on and discuss the journey in prayer program as a whole. Ask:

- Does anyone care to comment on the program?

- What have been the benefits for you?

- What can you do to continue your growth in prayer?

➤ 4. Begin the closing ritual with three minutes of silence during which people pray their breath prayer. (Use your watch or a timer.) After the silence, ask everyone to look around the group with an awareness of how blessed you are to be able to share your journey in prayer with one another. (Take a moment for everyone to look around.) Ask the group to turn to this page in their books. Together pray:

Thank you, God,
for bringing us together
on this journey into the life of prayer.
Light our way as we continue on
the path that takes us
closer to you.
Grant us the grace to feel
your presence
and to live out your call to
love one another as you
have loved us.
Amen.

NOTES

The BREATH of Life
▪ ▪ ▪
A WORKBOOK

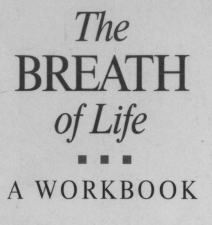

❖

*[The breath prayer]
is a way to have on our lips
what is always in
our heart.*

❖

JESUS SAID TO PRAY without ceasing, but how when the external demands and interruptions of life tug in thirty directions at once?

The Breath of Life Workbook enables individuals to join in groups to learn how to pray without ceasing. The simple five-week study offers a life-changing focus for individual prayer life.

The Breath of Life Workbook contains daily readings for five weeks, exercises in prayer and meditation, and other reflections to lead the individual into a deeper understanding of prayer. Through the easy-to-understand spiritual guidance of Ron DelBene, each reader will discover his or her own personal breath prayer.

Each day's reading includes
- a prayer
- guidance for one's personal prayer
- questions and exercises that encourage reflection and response

The Breath of Life Workbook offers a way to pray without ceasing and offers the abundance of life.

RON DELBENE holds a master's degree in theology and has done additional post-graduate work in education, psychology, and counseling. An Episcopal priest, Ron leads retreats, conducting events across the country in spirituality. With his wife, Eleanor, he directs The Hermitage, a nonprofit corporation devoted to providing opportunities in spiritual growth and pastoral care.

Ron and Eleanor live in Trussville, Alabama, and have two grown children, Paul and Anne.

MARY and **HERB MONTGOMERY** are full-time writers who have created numerous books and educational projects to help both children and adults grow in faith. The Montgomerys live in Minneapolis, Minnesota.

UPPER ROOM BOOKS

ISBN 0-8358-0766-5

9 780835 807661   90000